Weavers of Dreams

The Origins of the Modern Co-operative Movement

by
David J. Thompson

Center for Cooperatives • University of California

Table of Contents

Greetings by Arnold Bagnall, Mayor of Rochdale
Foreword by Bruce Thordarson, Director General,
International Co-operative Alliance
Introduction by Author

Revolution Comes to Rochdale 1

Robert Owen Sets the Stage for Co-operation 11

Chartism—People on the March 19

These Were the Worst of Times 27

The Night the Light Was Lit—The Weavers Open
   Their Store at Last 37

The Pioneers Make Progress 47

Champions of the Co-op 53

Co-op—The Pioneer of Pure Food 59

Cotton, Co-ops, and the U.S. Civil War (1861-1865) 65

Together They Build—Co-operation Among Co-operatives 75

The Revolution in Time—The Impact of the Stamp,
   the Newspaper, and the Train 87

The Basket That Changed Britain: The Successes
   of the Co-operative Women's Guild 91

Co-operative Education—The Road to Economic
   Freedom and Democracy 107

From Utopian Community to Garden City—
   Home Builder and Mortgage Banker 117

Toad Lane Yesterday and Today 135

Appendices

A. The Original Members of the Rochdale
   Equitable Pioneers Society Limited 141

B. The Original Statutes of the Rochdale Society of
   Equitable Pioneers and Today's International
   Co-operative Alliance Cooperative Principles 142

C. British Co-operative Movement Facts and Figures for 1994 145

D. International Co-operative Alliance Facts and Figures for 1994 146

Bibliography 147

Author's Biography 152

ROCHDALE
METROPOLITAN BOROUGH
COUNCIL

The year 1994 is the 150th anniversary of the modern cooperative movement. We all take great pride in the efforts of the Rochdale Pioneers to start their co-op at 31 Toad Lane. In that small shop one of the world's most important ideas was born. The Rochdale Pioneers showed us how ordinary people working together could be powerful. Combining the resources of people, capital and commerce earned them respect in the marketplace. What is so interesting is that the cooperative idea, born here in our town, has been exported to every corner of the earth.

This book, by David Thompson, deserves to be read. David is a Lancashire lad and his love for the co-op and Lancashire shows through on every page. His book is a rich history of the Rochdale Pioneers and of our town. As I read it, I was struck by the important role Rochdale played in ushering in the Industrial Revolution. What an era of economic and societal change. I felt anew after reading this book that there is nothing more enduring than people working hard to solve their problems.

As the years have gone by, the Museum at Toad Lane has become a Mecca for visitors from throughout the world. More visitors want to see the little shop than any other spot in town. The Rochdale Town Council works closely with the Cooperative Union to ensure the future of the Pioneer's building and the surrounding conservation area. We will continue to provide our international co-op friends with a fine place to come home to.

As Mayor, I often greet co-op visitors who have come to see Rochdale for themselves. I know how much No.31 Toad Lane means to all of you. This book becomes part of the record of their efforts and a reminder of their achievements. I continue to be impressed by the different types of cooperatives that abound in the world. Cooperatives continue to unite people together and solve common problems. I am sure the Rochdale Pioneers would be proud of what continues to be done in their name.

Allow me to wish cooperators here in Britain and around the world a successful anniversary year. On behalf of the Rochdale Council, you will always be welcome in the town which gave birth to your movement.

a Bagnall

His Worship the Mayor of Rochdale
Mayor's Parlour
Town Hall
Rochdale   February 1994

Foreword

The story of the Rochdale Pioneers, and their role in laying the foundations for today's worldwide Co-operative Movement, has been told before in many ways. To mark the 150th anniversary of the founding of the Rochdale Equitable Pioneers Society, David Thompson has chosen the approach of a true believer—a committed community developer who sees Co-operation as a means for achieving the twin goals of progress and equity.

The economic and social conditions facing the working class people of Northern England during the first half of the nineteenth century are recorded vividly here, and leave no doubt that Co-operation emerged, as it usually does, as a collective response to keenly felt needs. These were primarily economic needs, but to a significant extent they were also social—a desire for basic education, for political rights, and for more equitable participation of women. The Rochdale Pioneers, as Co-operative leaders after them have done throughout the world, were concerned with both economic and social forms of justice. They sought to combine the development of a strong, economic enterprise with contributions towards social and political reform.

What is striking from this account, in fact, is the extent to which the British Co-operative movement of the 19th Century exercised a significant influence on the development of national policies in such areas as consumer standards, women's rights, and popular education. The Co-operative

Women's Guild is described as "Britain's pre-eminent women's organization," and its parliamentary successes were significant indeed.

Like the author himself, the early Co-operative leaders were strong idealists. It is not surprising, therefore, that the door of the Rochdale store was painted a bright green—the symbol of the earlier Chartist Movement which had inspired many of the Rochdale Pioneers. But whether Owenites, Chartists, or Christian Socialists, the early leaders also realized the need to emphasize common values which would untie rather than divide their members.

As is well known, the Rochdale Society was not the first Co-operative in Britain. But, for a variety of reasons, it has become the symbol for a movement which is today worldwide and multi-sectoral. In large part, this is due to the Pioneers' wise and judicious financial policies. They emphasized the importance of member contributions to capital—as much as 10 weeks' wages—so as to avoid the problems of undercapitalized Co-operatives whose fate they wished to avoid. In order to attract this capital, the Co-operative paid a fair market rate, ranging from 3.5 to 5 percent. Equally important was its codification of the practice of dividends on purchases—both to ensure sufficient reserves for the Co-operative and to reward the individual member for his patronage. The wisdom of such policies remains apparent 150 years later.

When modern readers attempt to understand the reason for the success of the first consumer Co-operative, it is important to remember that its attraction was based not on price, which was related to the market, but rather on the values of quality and honesty. The attraction of "pure food" and "honest weight," combined with financial statements that were open to all members, demonstrated that the Co-operative was truly an alternative form of business operating in the interests of its users/owners.

Another characteristic of the early Co-operative leaders in Britain was their understanding of the need for vertical integration, not only in order to attain economics of scale for their consumer operations, but also to extend the benefits of Co-operation into other areas—manufacturing, farming, financial services, and education. The stories of the Co-operative Wholesale Society, the Co-operative Bank, the Co-operative Insurance Society, and the Co-operative Union have been told in detail elsewhere. For the purpose of this account, the important message is that attention to local matters—while essential—is not sufficient. Committed Co-operative leaders realize that their success ultimately depends upon a wider public understanding of co-operation, which in turn requires Co-operative action at both national and international levels.

This is certainly David Thompson's view, as attested by the attention which he pays to the efforts of the British Co-operative Movement to support both Co-operative education and housing. It is revealing that the Rochdale Society was allocating 10 percent of its profits to education (until the government's Registrar forced it to reduce this amount), and that it soon became "the foremost educational institute in Rochdale."

Today, some 150 years later, the concepts developed by the Rochdale Pioneers and their successors have spread around the world, joined and adapted by other philosophies and other cultures. The Co-operative model is today truly universal, but still reflects very much the values and principles which inspired the weavers of Rochdale. Their vision does indeed deserve to be celebrated in this anniversary year.

—Bruce Thordarson
Director-General
International Co-operative Alliance
Geneva, Switzerland

Introduction

By
David J. Thompson

This book is being published in honor of the 150th anniversary of the founding of the modern Cooperative Movement in Rochdale, England, in 1844 and the 100th anniversary of the founding of the International Co-operative Alliance in London in 1895. Writing this history has given me great personal enjoyment, and I am happy to bring to fruition a book I have wanted to write for the past ten years.

Having been born in Blackpool, Lancashire, and emigrating to the United States at twenty years of age, my life has been shaped by two countries and two cultures. For the past twenty years I have been involved in building cooperatives in the United States. As a result, this book also celebrates the many threads of cooperation that exist between Britain and the United States. At this time, the United States has the most vigorous and diversified cooperatives of any country in the world. Nearly 100 million cooperators have taken the idea of cooperation and made it a thriving part of the economy.

During the course of developing new cooperatives in the United States, I have been constantly reminded of the critical role of history. In particular, I have often revisited the sensibilities of the Rochdale Pioneers as they created the first modern cooperative. Their philosophy and practice set in motion standards that apply today. The Rochdale Pioneers tapped into the twin virtues of community and commerce, which, when successfully combined, lead to progress toward an equitable environment for all. Without that harmony, the world is cast into the haves and the have-nots and an unceasing struggle for dominance.

What drives me to write this history is my commitment to the philosophy and practice of cooperation. I believe strongly that the cooperative idea is economics on a human scale. Our world cannot work effectively when gross economic inequality persists among people. Humans cannot live healthy lives without community and sharing. The principles of cooperation make more sense today than ever before. Self-help is more effective than philanthropy, less costly than welfare, and a practical choice for many people.

Yet cooperatives continue to be misunderstood. Many governments either want to control cooperatives or avoid supporting them. Despite their proven track record as grass roots democratic organizations, the cooperative form of enterprise is frequently neglected, all too often because it gives power to the powerless. It is interesting to note that cooperation is the only major economic philosophy that has never had an army or a police force. Moreover, co-op leaders in Europe in this century were killed or imprisoned, first by the Communists and then by the Fascists. Even today, co-op leaders are being attacked and tortured in Latin America and Asia—all because they want people to own and operate their own businesses, serve their communities, and meet their own human and economic needs. This book has been written to promote hope and faith in the cooperative idea.

As a book, *Weavers of Dreams* has a number of goals. The first is to paint a picture of Rochdale and Lancashire that describes the lives and times of the Pioneers and the events leading up to the opening of their cooperative store. I would like the reader to understand what barriers the Pioneers had to break down in order to achieve success.

The other shopkeepers sneeringly designated the co-op as the "weavers' dream." It is also important to see that the Pioneers kept their eyes on the prize, calmly developing their co-op stores and leadership skills while all about them the world was in revolution. When reform finally came, the co-ops provided the leadership for the new democracy in Britain. Many of the newly-elected local officials forged their leadership skills at the co-op, making these co-ops the main training ground for modern democracy in Britain.

The second goal is to follow certain themes of cooperation which are just as critical today as they were in the 1840s—democratic control, the value of member education, the role and development of women, the search for unity and community, quality and purity of product, and the meaning of member capital, expansion, and cooperation among cooperatives.

The third goal of this book is to celebrate the success of the Pioneers. They showed the world that ordinary people working together and pooling their resources could achieve greatness. The co-ops were the first to successfully institutionalize national organizations to support local economic enterprises. The co-ops were a source of pride to the members. As the co-ops grew, they provided more services and took on more responsibilities. Time and time again, modern co-ops repeat past mistakes instead of learning from them. In every case, those co-ops that carefully follow the practical idealists from Rochdale have found success in their own time.

The fourth goal is to use the past to focus on the future. This year, 720 million people are using their co-ops to better their lives. More people than ever need to know how to build their cooperatives effectively to serve their needs. The successes created by the Pioneers and repeated by millions are the foundation for the future.

No writer of the history of the Rochdale Pioneers could pass up the opportunity to praise the work of George Jacob Holyoake's *The History of the Rochdale Pioneers,* and W. Henry Brown's *A Century of Co-operation in Rochdale.* Cooperative history is built upon their unforgettable writings. Two other books have been published in conjunction with the 150th anniversary of the founding of the modern Cooperative Movement—*Conflict & Co-operation: Rochdale and the Pioneering Spirit 1790-1844* by John Cole, a well-written, beautifully illustrated must for historians of the period, and *The People's Business* by Johnston Burchall which will be published at the Cooperative Congress in May. Burchall's other writings display his love for the Cooperative Movement, and this new book will assuredly be a seminal and attractive addition to cooperative literature. Given that the Principles will be modified at the International Co-operative Alliance Congress in Manchester in 1995, any further writing on them at this time would be outdated upon publication.

There are other areas where the contributions of giants cover the subject so completely that I could never match their scholarship. I commend to the reader a number of companion books which complete the story of the founding of the modern Cooperative Movement at Rochdale. In the area of cooperative principles, Paul Lambert's *Studies in the Social Philosophy of Co-operation*, William P. Watkins' *Co-operative Principles, Today and Tomorrow*, and Sven Åke Böök's *Cooperative Values in a Changing World* are recommended reading. For a discussion of the role of consumer versus producer cooperatives and the role of the worker in consumer cooperatives, there is no better book than Philip Backstrom's *Christian Socialism and Co-operation in Victorian England.*

Dedications

To my wife, Ann, for her love, unflagging support, partnership, and constant guidance on the path to completion of this book. To our daughter, Hatley Rose, our niece, Rayne, and our family around the globe for whom we build the future. To my parents, Una and Herbert Thompson, who taught my brother Philip and me to love Lancashire, to take responsibility for others, and to fight for those without rights. To Audrey Lippman for her constant support. To my cousins, Pat White and Vera Bond, for all of their help and hospitality while completing the research in Rochdale.

To those who by their example and commitment have personally inspired me on my own cooperative journey: Jerry Voorhis, Don Rothenberg, and Frank Sollars. To co-op educators, the co-op board members I have served with, my good colleagues at the National Cooperative Business Association, National Cooperative Bank, and the International Co-operative Alliance and to the staff of the Co-operative Union and the Pioneers' Museum. Finally, to my special co-op friends who dream the same dreams of a better world.

To my friends overseas, especially Messrs. Takamura, Ohya, and Kurimoto at the Japanese Consumers' Cooperative Union. To the dedicated cooperators and friends I have met throughout the world in China, Japan, Western and Central Europe, Russia, South Africa, Central and Latin America. Finally, the book is dedicated to the builders of the contemporary cooperative models throughout Japan, in the Basque region of Spain, and in the provinces of Quebec and Nova Scotia in Canada. Their commitment to institutionalizing development and building unified regional strategies gives us all hope and, more importantly, models. To all the cooperators whose daily life is committed to building a better world and better communities, I salute your efforts and urge you on to do as the Rochdale Pioneers—succeed in building cooperatives and hope!

I believe it is far easier to make history than to write about it. While I have done my best to accurately present the story of the Pioneers and their progress, the facts are not always agreed upon. When research findings have differed, I have made my own choices based upon my reading of the evidence. If any reader wishes to add to this evidence, comments are invited. The mistakes are my own and I welcome correction.

Finally, I wish to especially thank the following people whose supportive critique, keen eye, and historical scholarship were critical to development of the book: Doris Earnshaw, Roy Garratt, Dorothy Greene, Morrie Lippman, Robert Schildgen, Derek Shearer, Lloyd Wilkinson, and Ian Williamson. Ann Hoyt deserves particular credit for her thorough critique and valuable suggestions. Mahlon Lang and Bea Hoppes of the Center for Cooperatives and Marianne Post and staff of Repro Graphics at the University of California at Davis added invaluable support during the production process. Each person named has earned my gratitude for the time and talent contributed to this book.

Chapter 1

Revolution Comes
to Rochdale

*Nobody made a greater mistake than he who did nothing
because he could only do a little.*
— *Edmund Burke*

In 1844 events took place that heralded major economic change for the modern world. Three economic models, which have dominated the world economy for the past 150 years, took shape that year.

First, in 1844, the Joint Stock Act was passed by the British Parliament. This Act served as the key to the birth of modern capitalism by developing the basis for the modern stock corporation. Concurrently, Parliament passed the Bank Charter Act of 1844, which determined the constitution of the Bank of England and the role of a national bank in the economy. This Act completed the foundation of the nineteenth-century British banking and currency system. Therefore, at both a micro and a macro level, the structure of modern capitalism became an economic reality.

Second, in 1844, Karl Marx published *The German Ideology,* which developed the philosophical underpinnings of Communist thinking. It was the same year that Friedrich Engels, a German-born businessman and Chartist supporter then based in Manchester, wrote the classic, *Conditions of the Working Class in England.* The book came to the atten-

1

tion of Karl Marx, who then formed a lifelong association with Engels, beginning with the publication of *The Communist Manifesto* in 1848. By then, Engels had left to visit Marx in Paris and remained on the Continent to participate in the revolution of 1848. This intellectual association in 1844 not only gave birth to the theory of modern Communism but, most importantly, seeded working-class activism on a worldwide basis. Of *The Communist Manifesto*'s ten demands, six or seven are now law in most industrialized nations.

Third, twenty-eight working people founded the Rochdale Equitable Pioneers Society. A store was opened that offered only five items for sale, and though the shop lacked inventory, it was filled with hope. What they lacked in experience, the members made up with enthusiasm. From the mutual efforts of those humble workers grew an idea that today serves the needs of over 720 million members worldwide. The year 1844, therefore, represents the birth of the modern cooperative movement.

Rochdale, although historically a small town, holds an important role in the development of the Industrial Age of Britain. Astride the main road through the Pennine Hills leading between Lancashire and Yorkshire, Rochdale is situated at the entrance to Summit Pass. From time immemorial Celts, Vikings, Danes, and Romans were attracted to Summit Pass in northern England. It is one of only three low-level passes that lead through the Pennine Ridge, the hilly foreboding backbone of Britain. Portions of the old Roman road are still preserved as a public path through the pass. Traditionally, control of Summit Pass determined who controlled Northern England. The Pass connects the historically powerful counties of Lancashire and Yorkshire. This is the land of the War of the Roses, the struggle of the Red Rose of Lancashire against the White Rose of Yorkshire. Guarding the town is the Blackstone Edge, an abrupt hill looming over the important eastern entry into Rochdale. Running through the valley is the River Roch.

To enhance the growing trade coming through the Pass, the King granted Rochdale the right to hold a weekly market and annual fair in 1251. When Daniel Defoe, author of *Robinson Crusoe,* visited Rochdale in 1724 he found it "a good market town, and of late much improved in the woolen manufacture." Unfortunately, Defoe had to go over Blackstone Edge and the Pennines in a snowstorm. He later wrote, "The Town is situated so remote, so out of the way, and so at the very foot of the mountains, that we may suppose it would be but little frequented."

John Wesley visited the town in 1749 and spoke at the Wesleyan Chapel on Toad Lane. To the seekers of heavenly salvation Wesley urged such earthly practices as "buying one of another—helping each other in business," and to "gain all they can, and to save all they can." The Methodists and the Rochdale Pioneers later mastered both practices.

The historian Fishwick commented in 1777, "This town is remarkable for its many wealthy merchants; it has a large woolen market, the merchants from Halifax, etc., repairing hither weekly; the neighborhood abounds in clothiers . . ." The domestic wool trade was Rochdale's main activity until the first steam powered cotton mill appeared in 1790.

Riots and Revolts

However, world history was about to be turned upside down by the birth of the Industrial Revolution occurring across the southern Pennines. In the early 1700s, Rochdale was isolated, but by the early 1800s it was industrialized. Rochdale became one of the commercial centers for the growing woolen industry in Yorkshire and the cotton industry of Lancashire. The rushing streams of the Pennines brought cheap power to the busy mill towns of the bustling counties of Yorkshire and Lancashire. Rochdale was fortunate; it was equidistant between the mill towns along the Pennines and the cities of Liverpool and Manchester which shipped the processed cotton and wool cloth to the rest of the world. The town mirrored the vast changes occurring in the new industrial society.

In 1788 the first canal to connect Rochdale to the Yorkshire side was constructed. The canal obtained some of its water from the River Roch. By 1804, the 33-mile-long Rochdale Canal was open. It took ninety-two locks to get barges from one side of the Pennines to the other. Finally, there was a way to ship goods from the hills of South Yorkshire and the mills of South East Lancashire to the warehouses of Manchester and the port of Liverpool. For Rochdale the Industrial Revolution had begun; in 1801 the population was 11,000.

On 8 October 1829, *The Rocket* of George Stephenson, the father of railways, established a rail speed of 29.1 m.p.h. on the Liverpool & Manchester Railway. In March 1841, Stephenson built his famous Summit railway tunnel one and a half miles through the Pennines near Rochdale. The trains now stopped in Rochdale on their way between Manchester and Leeds. Forty-one lives were lost in the two years of construction. The last barrier to industrial progress in the North had been removed. By canal, road, and railway, goods, people, and ideas poured between the three Northern capitals of Leeds, Liverpool, and Manchester. As a result, Rochdale became a magnet for the major movements of an era of industrial development, working-class activity, and commercial transportation.

A brief look at the early 1800s shows why the changing times and events of the Industrial Revolution allowed Rochdale to become the birthplace of modern cooperation. In 1801, Britain had only 9 million people, which by 1851 had doubled to 18 million. In that same period, Manchester, the emerging industrial capital of Britain, grew from 85,000 to 400,000 people. Manchester became known as the "cottonopolis" of the world. Today, two and a half million people live within ten miles of Manchester's City Hall, making it the largest city in the north of England. From its 1801 population of 11,000, Rochdale is now home to 205,200 people.

However, all this change did not happen without conflict. Hundreds of thousands of people were on the move looking for work. A rural nation was transformed almost overnight into an urban society. Power looms were replacing the hand looms. The factory owners were consolidating production, and the weavers in their cottages were losing it. Conditions were ripe for revolt. Unemployment, near starvation, the poorhouse, disease and epidemics, child labor—all these were the lot of working people. The machinery went ever faster, the pay was never enough, the price of everything went up, and food was always too expensive. As a later chapter will show, these were the worst of times. England was often on the edge of an explosion.

In 1807, a massive petition from Lancashire weavers was presented to Parliament, asking for minimum wages and protesting wage reductions. The petition was rejected, and this action soon was followed by a strike. For two days, ten to fifteen thousand weavers gathered on St. George's Field, Manchester. The demonstrations ended with the killing of one man and the wounding of several others by troops.

In Rochdale, in 1808, the courthouse was burnt to the ground by rioters during the weavers' strike, which became known as the "Shuttle Gathering." The government sent one thousand soldiers of the Halifax Volunteers to be stationed in Rochdale to quell disturbances. They were followed by regular troops who were stationed there until 1846, housed for many of those years in barracks on Toad Lane.

Next followed the Luddite riots of 1811 and 1812. The Luddites, named after Ned Ludd, organized in Nottinghamshire, followed by South Yorkshire and then Lancashire. The Luddites were out to destroy the gig mills and wide knitting frames that threatened their future. All across the cloth manufacturing areas of the Midlands and northern England, workers rose up to smash the machinery. Twelve thousand soldiers were dispatched to put down the riots— more troops than Wellington had under his command when he defeated France in the Peninsula War. By 1813, fourteen rioters were hung and the Luddites disbanded.

The Reverend Patrick Brontë was then living in Hartshead, Yorkshire, in an area where cottage industry was giving way to factories. His recounting of the Luddite Riots to his children led Charlotte Brontë to write *Shirley,* her classic novel about industrial unrest in the North. The Brontës chronicled a great deal of life in the lonely Pennines, especially that around the bleak town of Haworth and the surrounding moors. The literate minds of the sisters made much of their surroundings. The best of the Brontës' writings occurred in the 1840s and 1850s, during the formative years of the Rochdale Pioneers.

In March of 1817, the radical leader Samuel Bamford

spoke to a large crowd in Rochdale. The meeting is regarded by local historian John Cole as "the first political reform meeting in the country." Political reform was the topic, one of great interest to an audience without any political power. In 1819, two weeks before the infamous Peterloo, a crowd of thirteen thousand gathered in Rochdale to petition for reform. Tom Collier, uncle of John Collier, one of the original Rochdale Pioneers, addressed the assembly. Tom Collier was the son of John Collier, creator of the great Lancashire dialect character "Tim Bobbin."

Peterloo

Later that year, on August 16, 1819, eighty thousand people—one of the largest crowds in British history to that date—demonstrated at St. Peter's Field in Manchester. The crowd represented 8 percent of Lancashire's population. They gathered to petition for the repeal of the Corn Laws and for the Reform Bill. Samuel Bamford led the contingent from Rochdale and Middleton to Manchester. Bamford wrote, "Our whole column with the Rochdale people would probably consist of 6,000." The banner carried high by Bamford and the Rochdale followers is the only one surviving from the Peterloo demonstration. On one side is the motto "Liberty and Fraternity"; on the other, "Unity is Strength." (It is displayed at the People's History Museum in Manchester.)

Bamford's account of that fateful day is still the most widely known. One reviewer, J. J. Bagley, comments that Bamford's fast-moving narrative carries the reader along so well that he senses the initial expectation and excitement of the Middleton men and women, falls in step with the drum beats, hears the cheering as procession passes through Blackley, Harpurhey, Colleyhurst, and the Irish district of Newton, and feels the rising tension as the Middleton contingent is absorbed into an ever increasing flow of people moving resolutely towards the meeting. By the time Bamford and his followers reach St. Peter's Field itself, the reader has become one of the demonstrators.

During an attempt to arrest the Peterloo leaders, confusion and panic erupted. The 15th Hussars, who had served at Waterloo, were ordered to charge the crowd, shooting broke out, eight people were killed and four hundred sent to the hospital, mostly as a result of stampeding horses. Two people from the Rochdale contingent were injured. Unfortunately for Bamford, he was arrested on charges of high treason along with nine others. They were taken to Lancaster Gaol and put on trial in March 1820. The leaders were found guilty, and Bamford was sentenced to one year in prison.

From that day on, because of the Hussars, the incident at Manchester has been referred to as Peterloo, a parody on Waterloo. It was the Duke of Wellington's victory at Waterloo in 1815 that had put an end to Napoleon, but the glories of a foreign victory were tied forever to the gloom of a domestic defeat. Peterloo was to make Manchester a center of continual dissent for many decades. The Manchester Free Trade Hall was purposely built on the site of Peterloo to permanently enshrine free speech in England. As a result of Peterloo, the liberal *Manchester Guardian* (now *The Guardian)* was founded two years later. At Peterloo the reformer voices of the industrial North began their demand for a different England.

Labour Begins to Organize

The Combination Acts of 1824 allowed workers to "combine" together to improve wages, but for nothing else. In 1834, a group of farmworkers in Dorset organized a union and were tried for administering illegal oaths. They had adopted their oath directly from the one used by the Rochdale handloom weavers to organize their union. The farmworkers were found guilty and transported to Australia. (In 1788, after England lost the American Revolution, it began shipping its convicts to Australia.) Known as the Tolpuddle Martyrs, their case and its severe sentences served to dampen open organization of workers for many years. It was not until 1868 that the Trades Union Congress dared to hold its first national meeting and Manchester was the chosen location.

In 1826 there occurred one of the most dramatic upheavals in the history of the cotton industry. Following in the footsteps of the Luddites, the Lancashire handloom weavers rioted across central and eastern Lancashire. During the month of April, bands of handloom weavers roamed from village to village destroying the new power looms. In four dramatic days, they destroyed eleven hundred power looms. Lancashire was seething with resentment against the new machines which were to put a generation out of work. Thousands took part in the spontaneous demonstrations, and thousands more cheered them on. However, the weavers, armed in most instances only with sticks and stones, were no match for the troops rushed to the scene. The rebellion died in the village of Chatterton along with the six weavers shot by the soldiers, who also left scores of wounded. Ten people were transported to Australia for life, and thirty others received jail terms.

The 1826 riots were to have a tremendous impact upon a young doctor in Manchester, James Phillip Kay. Born in Rochdale in 1804, he had gained direct knowledge of the effects of poverty. He determined that what was needed was not repression, but education about conduct and political economy. In 1833, he left a career in medicine to become one of the founding fathers of the English public education system and to make many lasting contributions to the people of Lancashire.

Another strike in 1829, the second "Shuttle Gathering," was put down by the local garrison and resulted in ten deaths, several prison sentences, and the deportation of Thomas Kershaw, one of the strike leaders. That same year, Feargus O'Connor addressed a political gathering at the Old Theatre on Toad Lane. O'Connor was the owner of the weekly Chartist paper, *The Northern Star*, which at its peak had a circulation of 30,0000 and cost four and a half pence. He was the self-styled champion of the unshorn chins, blistered hands and fustian jackets. People would gather at each other's houses to share in the cost of the paper and the news it brought them. O'Connor was a perennial favorite of the town, and the town traditionally a great audience for radicals and reformers. G. D. H. Cole, the labor historian, wrote, "Rochdale was next only to Manchester and Leeds as a center of working-class activity in the first half of the 18th century."

Reform is Too Little and Too Late
The Reform Bill was passed by Parliament in 1832. That

August two thousand people paraded victoriously through the streets of Rochdale. However, the patina of political reform covered up, for a moment, the paucity of power for working people. The Reform Act was a misnomer that manipulated the public's yearning for political participation. The Act failed to provide basic freedoms to the working class, and it once again denied them the vote. The Act had been expected to bring about many changes. It was instead a blow to the burgeoning democratic elements in society.

For example, out of Rochdale's population of twenty thousand people, John Fenton was elected the area's Member of Parliament (M.P.) with only 277 votes. He beat James Taylor, the Unitarian minister of what soon would be called the Co-op Chapel. Due to property and gender restrictions, only 632 votes total were cast for the three competing candidates, out of a population of 28,000. The Reform Act of 1832 increased the voting population of Britain only from 440,000 to 725,000. As a result, reform efforts turned again from political reform to industrial and economic organizing.

John Fielden, a nearby mill owner and M.P., wrote to John Cobden on November 16, 1833, "I am persuaded we are on the eve of important changes; the working people will not long submit to the chains with which they are enthralled; cooperative societies, trade unions, etc., exist in almost every manufacturing town and village . . ."

In 1833, factory inspections were introduced to England, and in 1834 slavery ended in British colonies. For a few years there was a slight respite from political action. By the end of the decade, however, political activity began heating up again. Resentment had been growing against the Corn Laws. Passed in Parliament in 1815 by the landowning aristocrats, the Corn Laws prohibited the importation of corn below a set price. The result guaranteed high profits for the lords and high prices of bread for the people. In October of 1838, the Anti-Corn Law Association was formed. On November 7 of that year, the Chartist leader Feargus O'Connor was back in Rochdale. He led a torchlight procession and spoke at a Chartist demonstration attended by two thousand people.

For two decades (1830 to 1850), the independent handloom weavers hung on in the villages of Lancashire.

They followed the Chartists in the 1830s, and then hoped for changes in the 1832 Reform Act. It was not until the 1850s that the weavers understood that the state would not be of any assistance to their plight. They adopted the practice of cooperation and the status of a joint stock company. The weavers pooled their resources and united in an effort to develop village factories. Through their worker-owned companies, they created work and paid themselves wages. In 1830, a group of handloom weavers formed the Rochdale Society, but there is little evidence of its progress. The story of the cooperative weavers is still hidden from history.

In the midst of the sea of change sweeping Britain occurred one of the milestones of the century. On June 26, 1837, the young Queen Victoria was crowned. It was a national holiday with great rejoicing in Rochdale, the nation, and the empire. The growth of the cooperative movement would parallel the immense changes associated with the Victorian Era. When Queen Victoria died in 1901, the sixty-third year of her reign, Britain's population had grown from 25 million to 40 million. The urbanization of Britain and the height of the British Empire occurred during her lifetime. On Coronation Day in 1837 she ascended to the throne amidst great ceremony. Amongst the poor workers of the North there was a pause to celebrate the glory of Britain. It was also a time to recognize that much more had to be done to better their lives. The next day they went back to work and to building their co-ops, unions, and friendly societies.

Chapter 2

Robert Owen Sets the Stage for Cooperation

If we cannot reconcile all opinions let us
endeavour to unite all hearts.
— New Harmony Gazette

Robert Owen (1771-1858) emerged in the early 1800s as the most important influence on the early cooperative movement. Owen's impact on British history is covered in hundreds of books, and he deserves far more study than can be given here. His roles as writer, speaker, philanthropist, factory reformer, educator, social reformer, and trade unionist were unsurpassed for someone of his day. In 1821, Owen first coined the term "cooperative society" in his magazine *The Economist. The Economist* (1821-1822) was devoted to Owenism and cooperation, a rather different perspective than today's *Economist* which was founded in 1843. Owen's motto of "Each for One and One for All" has been adopted by many organizations throughout the world, especially in Japan, where Owen and Owenism has a strong following.

Owen's initial influence grew out of his management of the mill town of New Lanark in Scotland. He had married the daughter of David Dale, a mill owner. Soon Owen took on management of the enterprise and built it into the largest cotton-spinning factory in Europe. Owen introduced a number of reforms into the factory, the community, and education.

His writings about society and about the need for new communities was to make him a celebrated figure in industrial Britain.

Owen had a commitment to bettering the life of the factory worker. He proved it through provision of housing with windows and fresh-air ventilation, healthy prepared food, education for all ages on-site at the mill, and good working conditions for all, especially young people. The resulting boost in productivity enabled him to have one of the most profitable mills in Europe. Leaders came from all over the world to see New Lanark and to marvel at Owen's success. From 1814 to 1824 there were 20,000 visitors to New Lanark. Today, New Lanark is one of Scotland's top tourist attractions with over 100,000 visitors annually and 400,000 annually expected by the year 2000. Owing to his success, Owen was invited to provide testimony on New Lanark to a committee of the House of Commons in 1816. His book, *A New View of Society,* published in 1817, was a best seller of its day and became one of the seminal books on community planning and industry. Recognizing its importance, John Stuart Mill, the philosopher, voluntarily corrected the book prior to publication.

For centuries, philosophers have set forth Utopian ideas. *Utopia* is the Greek word for nowhere, and it is generally used to describe a perfect place not yet found anywhere on Earth. Almost every Utopian community promotes a sense of equality and democracy, and resources and power are shared by all the citizens. It was not until the nineteenth century that this philosophy was put into practice. The work of Owen in Britain and the United States and that of Cabet, Fourier, Godin, and Saint-Simon in France, set the stage for community-building. From their writings and work, model communities emerged which affected the lives of real people. The organization of work, community, education, and health were all studied. The questions of who should own, who should profit, and who should decide were on the table. People everywhere in the rapidly industrializing nations of Europe were struggling for democratic control of their workplaces, their communities, and their nations.

In his work to build New Lanark as a model industrial

community, Owen needed other people's capital, since he was not a rich man. Owen took on a number of partners to finance New Lanark's growth and social programs. One of them, William Allen, a leading Quaker industrialist, in effect initiated the concept of socially responsible investing. To support Owen's community experiment, Allen and the partners agreed to provide capital at a limited return on investment, then set at 5 percent. Allen and others funded a number of colonies during the nineteenth century. The colonies required two elements: the support of a philanthropist and means to make the poor self-supporting. Owen's economic and social success was the subject of great discussion throughout the land, and it led to important parliamentary changes in industrial reform.

At New Lanark, Owen formed a company store that ploughed the profits back into the community. It was one of the few company stores not to take advantage of its customers. The store, along with most of the New Lanark Community, is now restored to its original splendor after a 10 million pound expenditure. A visit there will impress anyone with Owen's achievements. He cared for his workers more than anyone in Europe, and still made the greatest profit.

Owen's immense ability to capture the ear of leaders in Britain, France, and America lent credibility to his ideas. During the 1820s, Owen gave two separate addresses on his views of a new social system in the Rotunda of the U.S. Capitol. Attending on both occasions were the presidents—Adams and Monroe—their Cabinets, the Supreme Court, and both houses of Congress. In America, Owen is best known for his creation of the Utopian community at New Harmony, Indiana. From 1824 to 1829, the one thousand member community had tremendous impact upon the Utopian movement of the United States.

Owen was responsible for the first wave of British cooperatives, which lasted from 1830 to 1835. The goal of the Owenite co-ops was to finance communities in which the inhabitants could build a new society. Dr. William King of Brighton was one of those influenced by Robert Owen. Dr. King was befriended and sponsored in his efforts by Lady Byron, the divorced wife of Lord Byron, the poet, who became

13

a patron of Dr. King's cooperative efforts. In 1822, Lady Byron contributed the sizable sum of five pounds to the Cooperative Congress in Liverpool to sponsor an exhibition of goods being produced by cooperatives. Lord Byron was the last Lord of Rochdale, having sold his manorial rights in the 1830s. Unfortunately, Lord Byron preferred to use his legacy to promote revolution in Greece rather than reform in Rochdale.

King started a cooperative store in Brighton, but more importantly published *The Co-operator* (1828-1830). The paper had a wide circulation throughout Britain and a correspondingly large influence. James Smithies, one of the Pioneers, had a bound copy which he and the other Pioneers studied and discussed in depth. Many of the Rochdale Pioneers' themes were borrowed from Dr. King's writings.

One of Dr. King's disciples, William Bryan, a former secretary of the Brighton Cooperative Benevolent Fund Society, emigrated to America. He started the first co-op store in America in New York City in 1829 and maintained correspondence with his peers in Brighton, even though he had left under a cloud of suspicion about a portion of the co-op's assets. Bryan offered to sponsor the young sons and daughters of cooperators in Brighton to come to the New World to repay his debt of gratitude to the members. The membership of the new co-op never exceeded forty, and by 1830 the co-op had died without ceremony.

In 1830, sixty weavers formed the "Rochdale Friendly Cooperative Society." Many were affected by Owen's communitarian teachings, and they added those elements to their principles and practices. They had a small library of thirty-two books and sent a delegate, William Harrison, to the Birmingham Cooperative Congress of 1831. There were now hundreds of co-ops in Britain who sent delegates to the national congresses. In the same year, *The Manchester Guardian* reported that seven thousand people, one-third of the woolen weavers in Rochdale, were out of work. That year, the co-op's members had collected 108 pounds and were employing ten members. The members were "earning and learning" as they developed their co-op.

In 1833, the Society formed a co-op store at 15 Toad Lane,

which, though popular for a while, lasted only two years. They decided to divide the profits on capital invested. The rent for the house was six pounds a year. The small front room served as the shop, and the manager lived in the remainder of the house. The co-op felt compelled to keep extending credit to the members to compete with other shops. Being a membership co-op, they never felt that they could charge higher prices to cover the bad debts. Eventually the co-op could not cover its losses. Because it had not registered under the Friendly Societies Act, neither could the co-op legally sue the debtors in court. Charles Howarth, James Standring, and John Aspden were members of the co-op at 15 Toad Lane. Later they used the experience to develop the successful model created by the Pioneers.

Throughout Britain, Owenites started hundreds of co-op stores like the one in Rochdale. Many of them failed for the same reasons as 15 Toad Lane. Merging idealism with economic reality is a dogged task. Owen looked on these attempts at business with caution. Visiting Carlisle in 1836, he found ". . . to my surprise six or seven cooperative societies in different parts of the town, doing well, so they think. It is however high time to put an end to the notion very prevalent in the public mind that this is the social system which we contemplate or that it will form any part or arrangement in the New Moral World." William Lovett, who accompanied him on the journey, added, "But when he (Owen) found that great numbers among them were disposed to entertain many of his views he regarded them with more favour." Although there were some Owenite co-ops still in existence when the Rochdale co-op came into existence, they soon merged into the newer and more successful movement.

A small group of Rochdale reformers maintained their affiliation with the Owenite movement. They formed Branch no. 24 of the Rational Society, and in April of 1838 they acquired the use of an annex of the Weavers Arms, naming it the New Social Institute. In those days, pubs were the focal point of organized community life. Pubs gave birth to the friendly, sick, and burial societies that nourished the working class through hard times. The Weavers Arms was the birthplace and first headquarters of the Rochdale Pioneers, and it became a regular meeting place for the activists of the day.

Charles Howarth wrote to Owen on December 9, 1839 inviting him to speak in Rochdale, suggesting that " . . . they had been struggling to gain the support of public opinion," and that ". . . if you can come we are confident many of the middle and higher classes would attend to hear you." Howarth reminded Owen ". . . of the pledge you have so long been under to visit this town and it is most desirable for many reasons you do so. The public are continually inquiring when will Robert Owen the founder of your new system come to Rochdale. Hoping you will take this our request into your consideration and, by acceding to it you will very much oblige your admirers and followers in Rochdale and, in particular, your disciple Charles Howarth secretary." There is no record of Owen having replied. However, Robertson believes Owen spoke in Rochdale during the early part of the decade.

A number of Rochdale residents were involved in the last fling of Owenism, which succeeded in starting a series of communities throughout Britain. From 1840 to 1845, the Queenwood Community in Hampshire became the focus of Owen's efforts. By 1843, however, the Owenite branch in Rochdale had run out of steam, abandoned their meeting place, sold the furniture, and dissolved the branch. By 1845, Queenwood collapsed, and with it, the Owenite era. John Bent, one of the Pioneers, lost fifteen pounds in the community scheme. Among the Rochdale Pioneers receiving some of their money back from the Queenwood failure were James Smithies, George Healey, John Garside, William Mallalieu, and John Collier. Alexander Campbell, later one of the founders of the Scottish Cooperative Wholesale Society, was jailed for his debt incurred through his participation in the Owenite Orbiston Community in Scotland.

Owen left for America on August 23, 1844, only days after the first official meeting of the Pioneers, and stayed in the United States almost continuously until the summer of 1846. He was not, therefore, a witness to the events unfolding in Rochdale. Owen was seventy-three when the Pioneers opened their store, and seventy-six by the time he learned of its existence. He showed little interest in this second wave of co-op shops initiated by the success of Rochdale. Their success as retail enterprises meant little to him unless their ultimate and only goal was creating community.

Rochdale Almost Arrived in America

On December 29, 1849, James Daly, the Rochdale Pioneers' original secretary, died of cholera on board the *S.S. Transit* bound for America and was buried at sea. A native of Northern Ireland, he meticulously maintained the minute books of the society throughout the early years. Daly was a mathematician, musician, and prominent member of the Oddfellows Society, and he played an active role in getting the co-op going. As a joiner, he built the first set of shelves for the store. However, working, volunteering, and feeding a family of eight children in the "hungry forties" had been exhausting for the Daly family.

Daly, his wife (who died of cholera a few days later), and his children were on their way to Texas to start life again in the New World. Co-op members and Oddfellows had raised the money to send Daly to America.

There is no trace of where they were headed, although Texas was then the Mecca for many Owenites discouraged by the failure of the Queenwood Community. In his visit to America, Owen had favored the then quasi-independent Texas as a home for Utopian colonies. Mexico was also encouraging Utopian colonies. Owen discussed colonies in America with a French Utopian named Etienne Cabet during Cabet's exile in England (1834-39) and again on September 9, 1847, in London. After that meeting, Cabet decided to create a Utopia named Icaria in Texas. An advance guard of sixty-nine people departed for Texas on February 3, 1848. Several days later the French Revolution broke out.

While it is not known where James Daly was headed, he was bringing his talents to the New World to enrich the Utopian movement. America was full of opportunities for a practical idealist such as he. Blessed with meticulous note-taking and commitment, he was on his way toward making a difference. What a pity it is that this Rochdale founder perished before making his mark in the New World.

Owen's Contribution

To celebrate Owen's eightieth birthday in 1851, a public meeting was held at the John Street Institution in London. Owen exhorted the audience of nearly one thousand to direct their united efforts to "well educate, well employ, well place and cordially unite the human race." In the audience was Karl Marx, then living in London. Marx later wrote to Engels, "In spite of fixed ideas the old man was ironical and lovable." Both Marx and Engels were interested in the educational reforms initiated by Owen at New Lanark. In the 1870s Engels recounted that all social movements, all real advances in England in the interests of the working class were associated with Owen's name.

Owen's influence on the era was unquestionable. Whatever their political hue, activists were required to have an opinion on Owen's ideas. A few years before publication of *The Communist Manifesto* (1848), Friedrich Engels (1820-1895) was in contact with Owen. Their common concern about the ills of the industrial city engendered discussion. Were it not for the dramatic changes occurring in Europe, Lambert shows, there is evidence to suggest that Engels might have established an Owenite Colony in Germany in 1845.

Owen died in 1858, days after returning to his birthplace of Newtown in Wales. To commemorate his contribution to the cooperative movement, the Cooperative Union lovingly restored his grave in 1902. George Jacob Holyoake, the devoted Owenite who became the greatest missionary for cooperatives, was the main speaker at the graveside ceremony. Annually, hundreds of thousands of people from all around the world still make pilgrimages to Newtown, Wales; New Lanark, Scotland; and New Harmony, Indiana, to honor the work of Robert Owen.

Chapter 3

Chartism—People on the March

*There is nothing more difficult to take in hand,
more perilous to conduct,
or more uncertain in its success,
than to take the lead in the introduction
of a new order of things.*
— *Machiavelli*

The Chartist movement, although it was a political reform movement paralleled much of the same as Owenism. After the failure of the Reform Act of 1832 to extend democratic rights to all, the People's Charter became the focus for working-class political activity. The Charter was drawn up by William Lovett, a companion of Owen and an activist with the London Co-operative Society from 1832 to 1834. The Charter called for a number of items, including secret ballot, universal adult male suffrage, and no property qualifications for members of parliament.

One eyewitness, R. G. Gammage, had this memory of the numerous Chartist demonstrations:

> The processions were frequently of immense length sometimes containing as many as fifty thousand people; and along the whole line there blazed a stream of light, illuminating the lofty sky, like the

reflection of a large city in general conflagration. The meetings themselves were of a still more terrifying character. The very appearance of such a vast number of blazing torches only seemed more effectually to inflame the minds of speakers and hearers.

On Whit Monday in May of 1839, it was estimated that 200,000 people gathered to hear Chartist speakers at Peep Green in Lancashire. "Sell thy garment and buy a sword," proclaimed the Padiham banner.

The Charter presented to Parliament in London on July 12, 1839, was rejected by 235 votes to 46. James Taylor, a preacher from Rochdale's Unitarian Chapel (the Co-op Chapel), was a delegate to the Chartist Convention in London and voiced the town's support of the charter. Three days later, the Chartist Convention voted to call a general strike to begin on August 12 and last for what they called a "sacred month." Chartist meetings were held all across Britain to debate the virtues of a general strike. The Chartist leaders were placed under surveillance.

One such meeting was held in Rochdale in early August. Three months earlier, the Chartist paper, *Northern Star*, reported:

Chartists still continue to purchase arms in the towns and neighborhood. There is a village not far from Rochdale which contains 55 adult males, 45 of whom have each a rifle, and many of them pikes besides. The Chartists have commenced a run on the savings banks in Rochdale, which still continue at an amazing extent, they will have nothing but gold.

The fear of the Chartist movement among the growing middle class was evident. Although initiated to gain popular rights, the Chartist crowd often seemed on the verge of becoming a mob. Thomas Carlyle, the historian, had tried to awaken Britain's rulers to the arrogant mistakes of the French aristocracy. He wrote his *French Revolution* in 1837 to show how the French ruling class was unable to save itself by granting needed reforms to its people. In 1839, he wrote *Chartism* to urge the English ruling class to give the masses wise leadership and restore prosperity and tranquillity. In 1847 Carlyle came to Rochdale and visited John Bright, the Quaker activist, mill owner, and Member of Parliament. There they talked of the impact of Chartism and the popularity of *Mary Barton*, Elizabeth Gaskell's new novel about Chartism.

By August 1839, the Chartists remained undecided about holding a general strike, and speakers at meetings around the country voiced uncertainty about the next action. Feargus O'Connor, the firebrand Chartist leader, spoke again in Rochdale in 1840, and was jailed after a speech at a Chartist demonstration. In 1842, after a terrible winter of hunger and unemployment, 15,000 weavers descended on Rochdale and stopped the mills for several days. The Charter was presented to Parliament again in 1842 and again rejected. There were widespread Chartist riots fueled by the frustration of a powerless working class.

In the introduction to the Everyman edition of *Mary Barton,* Margaret Lane wrote:

> The novel with a social problem theme was a new and revolutionary development in the eighteen forties; yet Mrs. Gaskell seemed to have no misgivings. The character of John Barton, the hand loom weaver, a man of integrity and intelligence, early trade unionist and convinced Chartist, who in the struggle for justice is driven to commit murder took hold of the imagination from the start.

After the second defeat of the Charter, there appeared only two avenues open for further action. Either the Chartists could fashion an alliance with the middle class, which seemed impossible, or they could organize land colonies to create the two-pound minimum value of land ownership that gave male landowners the vote. In 1845, Feargus O' Connor split from the main Chartist movement and embarked on the latter course by establishing the Chartist Cooperative Land Society. His thrust for developing the Chartist colonies was to create a new and separate society and to gain the vote for colony members through their ownership of land.

Elizabeth Gaskell

No British novelist captured the Chartist era as well as Elizabeth Gaskell. She moved to Manchester in 1832, where she married an activist Unitarian minister. As a result, she was an everyday witness to the poverty of the times. Her novel *Mary Barton,* written in 1844, was the story of life in Manchester during the Chartist era. Elizabeth Gaskell had visited Rochdale to talk with the people about their demands for a new standard of life. She included in her book a poem by Samuel Bamford, who led the Rochdale contingent to Peterloo. Gaskell was attracted to the work of the Christian Socialists and their idea of worker cooperatives.

Chartism and the Pioneers

Since the north of England was the stronghold of the movement, many of the Pioneers had participated in Chartist activity. In 1834, O'Connor had been a popular candidate for M.P. of Oldham, the neighboring town to Rochdale. In Rochdale there was an active Chartist branch, and Sharman Crawford, the M.P., was pro-Chartist. Abraham Greenwood, who joined the Pioneers in 1846, was the Secretary of the Rochdale Chartist Association at age eighteen. Greenwood told *The Rochdale Observer* in an interview in 1900, "It started with the Chartists . . .It really was a social movement with the idea of bettering the conditions of the people." John Holt was treasurer for a time. David Brooks, John Kershaw, James Maden, James Manock, and John Scowcroft were all active Chartists.

Another Chartist who was a good friend to the Rochdale Pioneers was Thomas Livesy. Born in 1815, he was a contemporary of most of the Pioneers. He led many struggles at the local level to better the conditions of working people, especially those which extended the vote or local control. His favorite tactic was to organize public meetings around the issues of the day and use the lively working-class crowd to pressure the local M.P.s to be as radical as their nonvoting constituents. Livesy became a police commissioner in 1839, a position similar to a city council member today. James Standring, a Unitarian and a Pioneer at both the no. 15 and no. 31 Toad Lane co-ops, was also a commissioner. In 1840,

Livsey was elected to the Board of Guardians and became leader of the group opposed to the Poor Laws. As Livesy pursued working-class demands, he frequently clashed with John Bright who urged middle-class moderation.

From 1841 to 1843, Livesy was an active member of the group that was discussing development of a new Cooperative. In an 1841 article in *The Rochdale Spectator* about the history of the co-op, Ambrose Tomlinson, an active Chartist and cooperator, describes how the members began collecting money for their newest endeavor. By February 7, 1843, they had entrusted to Alderman Livesy the sum of over eight pounds. He agreed to hold the shares in trust for the co-op group, which preceded the Pioneers.

Later, in the 1901 *Rochdale Household Almanac*, Tomlinson stated, "Co-operation originated not from a weavers' strike but from the old Chartist Movement. The Chartists had begun to hold meetings in a room at the corner of Penn Street. At these meetings Co-operation was talked about. The secretary was Thomas Livesy . . . They were discussing Co-operation in 1841, and in 1842 some of the members began to pay three pennies per week in order to accumulate funds in connection with a Cooperative scheme. . . After a while there was a quarrel, the Co-operators in the Society seceded and some of them were amongst the members of the Pioneers' Cooperative Society."

In the 1850s, Livesy became one of the Arbitrators for the Pioneers, a position signifying great trust and respect. When he died, he was given the greatest funeral that Rochdale had ever seen.

In 1848, Samuel Ashworth, one of the Pioneers, was still listed as an owner of two acres in a Chartist colony, along with a Mr. Edmund Kershaw (a Pioneer surname) and Mr. B. Sleddaw, both of Rochdale. Both Miles and Samuel Ashworth went to live in Charterville for a time, but Sam returned to Rochdale after six months. O'Connor made them converts during his visit to Rochdale in 1843. Many of the Pioneers crowded into the Old Theatre on Toad Lane to hear O'Connor speak about better living on the land in Chartist colonies. Meanwhile, William Cooper continued practicing gardening at home in preparation for life at the colony. Fortunately, he resisted life on the land and stayed to become one of the great co-op stalwarts.

O'Connor always found a great audience waiting for him in Rochdale. On August 2, 1846, O'Connor and Ernest Jones (later to be a great co-op leader and writer) addressed ten thousand people on Blackstone Edge. It was a natural amphitheatre for their adulation. The foreboding Pennine moor overlooking Rochdale was covered in Chartist supporters.

Chartism's Final Hour

The Corn Laws, which drove up the price of bread by taxing imported grain, were repealed in 1846. Workers finally found themselves taken seriously. Many Chartists stood for Parliament in the elections of 1847 and won. Among the winners was Feargus O'Connor, who stood for Nottingham in the Midlands. With the French Revolution of 1848, feelings rose high again: a new Chartist convention was summoned, a new petition was prepared. Once again, however, there were the old obstacles of diverse aims and insufficient organization, not to count the very capable spies planted by the government. Kennington Common in South London was the site of the Chartist rally. The people of London gathered anxiously awaiting word. Would the Chartists choose to rally or revolt? Was the year of European revolution to spread to Britain? Would the capital be in flames before the night was over? A nation stood on edge wondering whether the revolts occurring in 1848 in most European capitals would be repeated in London.

In the end, pouring rain dampened the crowd's spirits and the massed soldiers sobered their minds. Even Samuel Bamford, the old time Radical, was drafted as a constable and sent to Kennington Common to help maintain order. Charles Kingsley and F. D. Maurice, both ordained ministers, rushed to London to try to head off revolution. Kingsley immediately drafted a placard which was posted all over London. He counseled the Chartists to "be wise, and then you must be free, for you will be fit to be free." He wrote home on Monday, April 10 ". . . All is right as yet. Large crowds, but no one expects any row, as the Chartists will not face

Westminster Bridge . . . and are going to send up only the legal number of delegates to the House (of Commons)." The Charter was presented and subsequently rejected. The deed had been done, the day was over. As the Chartists trudged home in defeat, London breathed a sigh of relief.

The year 1848 signaled the end of an epoch. Europe stood at a precipice and nearly jumped. New forms of struggle replaced the old. Both worker and industrialist advanced in sophistication and retreated from raw power and armed struggle. Combat moved to other fields. The Chartists had had their day. Others were now getting ready to take their place.

While O'Connor attracted thousands of people to support the Chartist colonies, the idea had many financial flaws, and by the late 1840s it had failed. In 1851 the Chartist land scheme was wound up by Act of Parliament. It left in its wake thousands of working people who had placed their dreams and their money in O'Connor's hands. Bravely, Sharman Crawford sat on the Parliamentary Committee that took control over the mess. It took seventy years to untangle the ownership of land in the five colonies established under the Chartist land scheme. To O'Connor's credit, almost all of the buildings erected are lived in today.

Although its supporters were disappointed in the failure of Chartism, the movement towards democracy forged on. Many Chartists provided important leadership in the growing cooperative movement. In 1852, co-op leaders in London initiated a series of lectures to educate the interested public about their plans. Several prominent reformists addressed the meetings, including Bronterre O' Brien, regarded as the ablest leader of Chartism. Twenty years previously, O'Brien, like O'Connor, a fiery Irish speaker, had addressed the Second Cooperative Congress of 1832. Throughout his life, O'Brien supported the ideas of Owen and economic democracy. He believed that the most rapid change in society would only come about through extending the vote to everyone.

In his 1850 novel, *Alton Locke*, Charles Kingsley writes about the life of a tailor who becomes a Chartist. Locke is asked, "So you are a Chartist still?" Locke replies,

If by a Chartist you mean one who fancies that a change in mere political circumstances will bring about a millennium, I am no longer one. That dream is gone—with others. But if to be a Chartist is to love my brothers with every faculty of my soul—to wish to live and die struggling for their rights, endeavoring to make them, not electors merely, but fit to be electors, senators, kings and priests to God and to his Christ—if that be the Chartism of the future, then am I sevenfold a Chartist.

By 1850, an era of revolutionary protest had run its course. The effort had been costly for the thousands of British working class people who had been imprisoned, fired, intimidated, or attacked. From 1801 to 1835, 472 convict ships sailed to Australia. *The Fatal Shore* by R. Hughes tells the story of the convicts' lives after arriving at the other end of the world. Many were transported for life rather than hanged in England for political or protest crimes.

In 1890, an "Old Chartists" gathering took place in Rochdale and was attended by thirty of the townspeople. The participants reminded each other of the stirring times Chartism had created in the 1840s. Because of their struggle, Britain's power structure had been changed forever. The aristocracy had been replaced by the new captains of industry, the conservatives by the liberals, and a new progressive force had appeared. After a long and hard struggle, ordinary people who organized brought modern-day freedoms to the people of Britain.

Chapter 4

These Were the Worst of Times

Revolts grow from the anger of people;
movements grow out of their hopes.
—Jack Bailey
British Cooperative Movement

How little can the rich man know
Of what the poor man feels,
When Want, like some dark demon foe,
Nearer and nearer steals!

He never tramp'd the weary round,
A stroke of work to gain,
And sicken'd at the dreaded sound
Telling him 'twas in vain.

Foot sore, heart sore, he never came
Back through the winter's wind,
To a dark cellar, there no flame,
No light, no food to find.

He never saw his darlings lie
Shivering, the grass their bed;
He never heard that maddening cry,
"Daddy a bit of bread!"
—Manchester song of the early 1800s

In 1839, half of all funerals in London were for children under ten years of age.

Robert Southey, the Poet Laureate, visited Manchester in 1808 and was horrified not just by the poverty. He was shown round one mill by the owner, who pointed proudly to the youngest of his work-force.

"You see these children sir," said he, "they get their bread almost as soon as they can walk about, and by the time they are seven or eight years old bring in money. There is no idleness amongst us; they come at five in the morning, we allow them half an hour for breakfast and an hour for dinner; they leave work at six and another set relieves them for the night; the wheels never stand still." Southey did not argue with his host. "I listened without contradicting him for who would lift up his voice against Diana at Ephesus?"

At some manafactories [sic], married men having families, are working six full days, and four nights, till nine and ten o'clock, for seven, eight, and eleven shillings a week. The very highest wages, of the swiftest men at such manafactories, are never more than thirteen shillings a week, for fifteen or sixteen hours a day, of intense labor.

Lads, from sixteen to twenty years of age, are working fifteen hours a day, for two shillings, half a crown and three shillings a week. Females from sixteen to twenty years of age, are earning two to three shillings a week; the hours of labor being from twelve to fifteen hours per day.

—The Co-operator
Vol. 2, June 1828

Robertson described life in Rochdale in the late 1830s to early 1840s:

The working class of Rochdale at this period were

very poor, and their chief purchases were meal and
coarse flour. Four years previous to this date (1836)
180 beasts were killed weekly in the parish of
Rochdale, and in 1841 the number was reduced to 65
or 70. Good joints were difficult to sell, and customers bought a pennyworth or two pennyworth of suet,
or bits of steak. Drs. T. H. Wardleworth, Robert
Barker, George Morris, and Walter Dunlop (local
medical gentlemen and owner of 31 Toad Lane), gave
it as their opinion that, owing to the high price of
food, and the want of employment, the labouring
classes in Rochdale at that time were suffering great
and increasing privations; that great numbers were
unable to obtain wholesome food in sufficient quantity to maintain them in health; and that they were
predisposed to disease, and rendered unable to resist
its attacks; that many cases of appalling distress and
suffering came almost daily under their notice. They
added that the population were in a much worse position then than they were five or six years before,
and that for three years past their condition had
been gradually sinking, and that they never knew
them in so bad a state at any former period.

In the 1840s, people had to pay twenty-four to thirty-six
pennies per week for two rooms. Deduct that from the average wage of 120 pennies per week for a 60-hour work week.

James Standring was the Secretary of the Rochdale Ten
Hours Committee, and he and Charles Howarth often went
to London to testify on behalf of the Ten Hour legislation.
Howarth was sent to London by the cotton operatives to meet
M.P.s and to watch the progress of the Factory Act. The Act,
which limited working hours to a ten-hour day, was passed
by Parliament in 1847, and Howarth was there to see it
passed.

Engels followed the Ten Hours' Bill closely.

Let us take some of the statements of a speech with
which Lord Ashley introduced the Ten Hours' Bill, 15
March 1844, into the House of Commons. Here he
gives some data as to the sex and age of the opera-

tives, not yet refuted by the manufacturers, whose statements, as quoted above, cover moreover only a part of the manufacturing industry of England. Of 419,560 factory operatives of the British Empire in 1839, 192,887, or nearly half, were under eighteen years of age, and 242,296 of the female sex, of whom 112,192 were less than eighteen years old. There remain, therefore, 80,695 male operatives under eighteen years, and 96,569 adult male operatives, or not one full quarter of the whole number. In the cotton factories, 56 1/4 per cent; in the woolen mills, 69 1/2 per cent; in the silk mills, 70 1/2 per cent; in the flax-spinning mills, 70 1/2 percent of all operatives are of the female sex. These numbers suffice to prove the crowding out of adult males. But you have only to go into the nearest mill to see the fact confirmed. Hence follows of necessity that inversion of the existing social order which, being forced upon them, has the most ruinous consequences for the workers. The employment of women at once breaks up the family; for when the wife spends twelve or thirteen hours every day in the mill, and the husband works the same length of time there or elsewhere, what becomes of the children? They grow up like wild weeds; they are put out to nurse for a shilling or eighteenpence a week, and how they are treated may be imagined. Hence the accidents to which little children fall victims multiply in the factory districts to a terrible extent. The lists of the Coroner of Manchester showed for nine months: 69 deaths from burning, 56 from drowning, 23 from falling, 77 from other causes, or a total of 225 deaths from accidents, while in non-manufacturing Liverpool during twelve months there were but 146 fatal accidents.

Sharman Crawford, the Rochdale M.P., said that of the people who lived in Rochdale in 1841, "136 people lived on six pennies per week, 200 on ten pennies, 855 on eighteen pennies, 1,500 on not more than twenty-two pennies. One-eighth of the population lived on less than fifteen pennies a week."

A comparison with the conditions of today highlights the conditions of the 1840s. In 1980, 1.8 percent of all male deaths and 1.4 percent of all female deaths were children under five years of age. In the 1840s, 40 percent of all male deaths and 41 percent of all female deaths were children under five years of age. For women who reached the age of twenty-five, 46 percent died before they reached the age of forty-five. In 1980, the corresponding figure was 2 percent. In only 4 percent of all cases did women in the 1840s reach the age of seventy-five, whereas in 1980 the figure was 60 percent. In 1840, the average life expectancy of a Manchester laborer was seventeen, whereas a Rutland landowner could expect to live to fifty-two.

Once again, Engels paints a bleak picture of conditions in 1844.

The great mortality among children of the working class, and especially among those of the factory operatives, is proof enough of the unwholesome conditions under which they pass their first years. These influences are at work, of course, among the children who survive, but not quite so powerfully as upon those who succumb. The result in the most favourable case is a tendency to disease, or some check in development, and consequent less than normal vigour of the constitution. A nine-year-old child of a factory operative that has grown up in want, privation, and changing conditions, in cold and damp, with insufficient clothing and unwholesome dwellings, is far from having the working strength of a child brought up under healthier conditions. At nine years of age it is sent into the mill to work 6 1/2 hours (formerly 8, earlier still, 12 to 14, even 16 hours) daily, until the thirteenth year; then twelve hours until the eighteenth year.

It was not until 1833 that the first Factory Act made it illegal to employ children under nine, or for women and those under eighteen to work more than twelve hours per day. Sixty years were to pass before another act dealt with health and safety at work.

31

In her report to the Cooperative Congress of 1892, which was held in Rochdale, Beatrice Potter presented some findings that she derived from the Parliamentary Reports of 1870. The children of Rochdale were not able to receive a fair start in life because their mothers all too often went to work in the mill while their children were still in the cradle. At ten years old, the Rochdale child was one and a half inches shorter and five pounds lighter than the average British school child, and was three and a half inches shorter and weighed eleven pounds less than the average. Rochdale children entered the factory at ten instead of the standard age of twelve.

Free Trade, Corn Laws, and the Right to Vote

The road to political and economic reform took many turns, but its beginnings were associated with the Industrial Revolution and the growing demands of the working class. The combination of high food costs due to the Napoleonic Wars and the effect of the protectionist Corn Laws, the abuse of the factory system, and the squalid living conditions necessitated reform. As you can see, Rochdale was in the thick of things.

Emigration was one of the few options for those seeking economic security and freedom. It is estimated that between 1770 and 1890 eleven million people crossed the Atlantic from Great Britain to the United States. Many left Rochdale for every corner of the world. In the United States, a woolen manufacturing center grew up in central Massachusetts. Some of the mill owners and many of the mill workers came from Rochdale and brought their skills to the New World. Founded in 1869, the village is the only place in the United States bearing the name Rochdale.

The origins of many of the cooperatives in the United States are tied to the presence of immigrant cooperators from Britain who brought their Owenite, Chartist, reformist, and cooperative practices from the Old World to the New World — they simply swapped continents.

Richard Cobden, a great radical leader and father of the "Free Trade Movement," was M.P. for Rochdale in 1859. It was Cobden's idea in 1850 to create Freehold Land Societies to gain people the right to vote. The society would buy freehold land and split up the ownership into parcels just large enough to give the new owner the right to vote. The Rochdale Freehold Land Society, founded in the same year and led by the Quaker John Bright, added five hundred new voters, almost doubling the electorate. Bright helped raise ten thousand pounds to buy twenty-four acres of land, which was then divided into five hundred lots. Each owner gained the right to vote.

From 1838 to 1846 Cobden fought unsuccessfully to repeal the Corn Laws and adopt policies of free trade that would give British workers and consumers access to food and products from abroad without protectionist taxes. Protectionist laws added taxes that doubled or tripled the real cost of many foods. Prior to the reintroduction of income tax in 1842, taxes, customs, and duties on food provided half of total tax revenue for Britain.

John Bright led the Rochdale branch of the Free Trade Movement, and in 1840 he obtained 9,750 names on a petition to repeal the Corn Laws. The petition presented to Parliament from Rochdale was 170 feet long. In December of 1842, Cobden and Bright both spoke at a rally of the Anti-Corn Law League at the Old Theatre on Toad Lane. The rally raised spirits and, more importantly, the grand sum of 1,700 pounds for the League's funds.

A Lancashire mill owner and M.P., Sir Robert Peel, abandoned his support for the Corn Laws in 1841 and carried the repeal laws in 1846. The Irish Famine caused by the failure of the potato crop in 1845 and bad harvests in Britain set the stage for repeal. Peel first became Prime Minister for a few months in 1834, and then again from 1841 to 1846. Repeal of the Corn Laws split the Conservative Party.

As leader of the repeal movement, Peel and his followers joined with the Whigs to form the embryonic Liberal Party. The new grouping was committed to free trade, religious tolerance, and Irish Home Rule. Together they brought about a series of major reforms of the British political and economic system. Peel was twenty-one when he first entered Parliament. He is remembered often as the father of the modern London police force. To this day, the slang for the English police is "bobbies" or "peelers." Sir Robert's life is commemorated by a stained glass window lighting the grand staircase of the Rochdale Town Hall.

Dickens' Christmas Carol—A Prelude to the Pioneers

Charles Dickens probably drew the best literary picture of how life was lived in the 1840s. His great novel *A Christmas Carol*, was published on December 19, 1843, a year — almost to the day — before Toad Lane opened its doors. Is there anyone who cannot immediately conjure up a picture of Bob Cratchit, Tiny Tim, Ebenezer Scrooge, and the ghost of Silas Marley? The other side of England that Dickins depicted in *A Christmas Carol* accurately describes Rochdale's Christmas of 1844. Dickens wrote the book in six weeks. The book set the stage for Dickens' secular humanistic theme to become the model holiday celebration in the English-speaking world. Dickens saw everyone as part of the same family. Harmony and unity were two of his most important themes, and, through them, the world could have a happy ending.

A visit to Manchester was a major inspiration for *A Christmas Carol*. In the summer of 1843 Dickens journeyed to the north of England. There he made a speech at the Manchester Athenaeum, a local institution dedicated to providing working men with an education. In his speech Dickens declared that ignorance itself was "the most prolific parent of misery and crime." He then urged that employers and employees come together and share "a mutual duty and responsibility." One week later on his return to London, Dickens began to develop the idea for *A Christmas Carol*. Dickens was thirty-one when he wrote *A Christmas Carol*. By that age he had become the most popular author in the English-speaking world.

The book thrust him onto the world's stage. However, his own life had colored the story. His father had been thrown into debtor's prison, and, at the age of ten, Dickens had been put to work in a crumbling warehouse by the Thames earning eighty cents a week. Dickens later wrote, "No words can express the secret agony of my soul . . . of being utterly neglected and hopeless; of the shame I felt in my position; of the misery it was to my young heart . . ."

On the eve of a revolutionary era which peaked in 1848, Dickens' message was that hearts had to change if society was to change. Dickens' philosophy would soon be challenged by another author. In 1849, Karl Marx moved to the same London neighborhood as Dickens. While Marx appreciated Dickens' literary skills, he was convinced that society would only change with the rise of the working class. As Marx said, "Philosophers have interpreted the world in various ways, but the point however is to change it." Change without revolution was almost impossible for Marx to imagine. The two authors took different paths and had different dreams for a better world.

Chapter 5

The Night the Light Was Lit!
The Weavers Open Their Store at Last

And the humble cooperative weavers of Rochdale, by saving two pennies when they had none to spare, and holding together when others separated, until they had made their store pay, set an example which created for the working-classes a new future.
— George Jacob Holyoake

The store first opened from 8 p.m. to 10 p.m. on Saturday evening, December 21, the winter solstice, the longest night of the year. Darkness arrives by 5 p.m. in this part of northern Europe—along with temperatures in the low thirties. The damp, foggy night air would bring a chill to anyone's bones. It was St. Thomas' Day, the saint also known as "Doubting Thomas." Under the old Gregorian calendar, adopted less than a hundred years earlier, December 21 was Christmas Day. Could the evening have been any more symbolic for the start of the modern cooperative movement?

James Smithies took down the shutters from the windows for the first time, and without fanfare the co-op was open. The honor of selling the first item was bestowed upon nineteen-year-old Samuel Ashworth. He was so nervous and inexperienced that, after seeing him struggle to wrap the pound or so of sugar in paper, the first customer decided to carry the sugar home in her apron.

The loyal members stood inside the shop huddled together for warmth and companionship. They shuffled their wooden clogs on the cold flagstone floor, watching their breath float across the candlelight. The windows were covered in damp, so no one could see outside. The sound of clogs clattering along the cobbled streets was their only guide to the arrival of a customer. All too often the sound of those clogs rushed past the store and disappeared into the distance like a passing train. Yet a few brave and loyal souls ventured through the door, and their humble purchases helped make history. Spirit furnished the members' capital, hope provided their inventory, hearts nurtured community, while their minds focused on their future.

Holyoake described the presence of the "doffers" at the door on opening night. The "doffers" were the young factory boys who loved to bring mischief wherever they gathered. "On the night when the store was opened, the 'doffers' came out strong in Toad Lane peeping with ridiculous impertinence round the corners, ventilating their opinion at the top of their voices, or standing before the door, inspecting with pertinacious insolence, the scanty arrangement of butter and oatmeal—at length they disclaimed in chorus, "Aye! the owd weavers shop is opened at last."

In Rochdale, the Pioneers could not afford to philosophize. They had mouths to feed, work to do, and money to raise. In Rochdale the almost barren shop opened four days before the Christmas of 1844. Here, looking at the empty shelves, the Pioneers were searching for change more real than Dickens' warm feelings and less horrific than Marx's revolution. Hopefully, the happy response of Tiny Tim to the troubled world around him would also uplift the spirits of the Pioneers: "God bless us every one."

The Pioneers Prepare

The Pioneers began operations in the front room with sixteen pounds, eleven shillings and eleven pennies left to spend on inventory after paying for some improvements. David Brooks was the first purchaser appointed by the society. He made eighty-four to ninety-six pennies a day at his regular job, but frequently left to earn three pennies per hour working for the co-op. Brooks purchased twenty-five pounds of butter, fifty-six pounds of sugar, six sacks of flour, and one sack of oatmeal for the Pioneers' opening night. The store opened with five items for sale: sugar, flour, oatmeal, butter, and tallow candles. The board meeting held on December 12 had approved the first four items.

However, the Pioneers were forced to buy two dozen tallow candles on opening night because the gas company refused to supply gas for the lights. The Pioneers soon realized that they could buy candles cheaper by purchasing in bulk and selling what they did not use. Samuel Ashworth, the son of the first president, was appointed salesman, and Thomas Cooper was named cashier to open the store and serve as shopman. If the store did not show a surplus in the first three months, they agreed to take nothing for their service. However, if it was able to pay a dividend, they were to receive three pennies per hour, which amounted to nine pennies per night. The salary of a permanent night shopman was to be set at fifty-four pennies per week.

In the beginning the shop opened only two nights per week from 8 to 10 p.m. In March of 1845, the store hours were set for Monday 4 to 9 p.m., Wednesday 7 to 9 p.m., Thursday 8 to 10 p.m., Friday 7 to 9 p.m., and Saturday 1 to 11 p.m. In April of 1851 the store began operating during the day. When the weavers and their families turned up on December 21, 1844, they found the door had been painted the same shade of green used by the Chartists. The co-op's storekeepers wore sleeve bands of the same color. The Pioneers may have given up on any hopes of Chartist success, but they would not so easily give up Chartist symbols. It was probably Miles Ashworth, a Chartist supporter, who painted the door. In 1993 the door was repainted again in Chartist Green in preparation for the co-op's 150th anniversary.

In Britain there was a long sequence of cooperative efforts aimed toward relieving the suffering imposed by the Industrial Revolution. One of the earliest occurred in 1760, when a group of workers opened their own corn mills at Chatham and Woolwich. Later, in 1797, another worker-owned mill opened in Hull. In 1816 the Sheerness Economical Society established its own bakery. These early efforts all focused on lowering the cost of bread, the main food staple, through production activities. Consumers were not able to grow wheat, nor were they in a position to mill the flour or mass bake the bread to reduce cost. For centuries in Europe there was a direct correlation between the price of bread and the outbreak of revolts.

Up in Scotland, the Fenwick Weavers opened a store in 1769, the Govan Victualling Society was founded in 1777, and the Lennoxtown Cooperative Society was formed in 1812. The last co-op is credited with operating on a system of paying a dividend on purchases. Alexander Campbell, the Scottish Owenite, claims to have developed the concept before Charles Howarth. A similar co-op in England called the Oldham Cooperative Supply Company opened in 1795. Each one of these retail cooperatives was focused on local relief and not on developing an alternative economic system or Utopian community.

It is more than a mere historical note to mention that the Joint Stock Companies Act of 1844 was in place when the Rochdale Pioneers were looking at registering. This new act and related subsequent legislation are seen as one of the foundations of modern capitalism. These acts introduced the concept of legal liability, which meant that investors were at risk in a corporation only to the extent of their investment. Prior to the act, investors in companies were personally liable for all the debts of the corporation. Up until then, only the very rich could afford to form corporations. This act created opportunity for small firms and investment possibilities for the growing middle class. The foundation for modern cooperation, communism, and capitalism was established in the same year.

In 1843 there was a great strike by the flannel weavers of Rochdale. The strike failed, causing great distress throughout the town, and the weavers began to look for other ways to better their lives. John Kershaw, one of the original Pioneers recounted:

> In the summer of 1843, Rochdale was placarded, announcing a discussion on "The best means of obtain-

ing the People's Charter." I attended that discussion; so did Charles Howarth, James Smithies and James Daly. It was there I first heard the principles of the Pioneers announced. Charles Howarth taking the lead, was well supported by Smithies, Daly and others. Mr. Howarth showed, as I thought very clearly that it was the only lever by which the working-class could permanently improve their social and political condition. His scheme and its details were so well studied out, and clear that it commanded assent. It was said at this meeting that a cooperative society had been in existence in Rochdale not more than two years before, and that it had gone down. Howarth at once showed us the reason why. He seemed thoroughly acquainted with the cause, and was well prepared with a new principle which would keep continually infusing new life into the movement.

The debates were usually held in the Rochdale Temperance or Chartist Room on Sunday afternoons. At a later meeting, held at the Weavers Arms during Christmas of 1843, John Kershaw asked Howarth how long it would take to get the land and workshops under the control of the workers if they each invested three pennies a week and allowed all the profits to accumulate to the cooperative so it could grow. At the next meeting Howarth presented a paper showing that working men would become their own employees in fifteen years if they invested in the co-op, gave their loyalty to the store, and did not take profit.

Robertson recounts the next steps of the Pioneers:

Again and again was discussed the advisability of starting a cooperative store, where goods could be sold free from adulteration and at reasonable prices, and by some then unsettled means, the profit, after paying all expenses, to be distributed amongst the members. At times their enthusiasm rose very high, and their faith in the scheme was very strong; but sometimes their spirits were depressed, especially when they remembered how the former store had failed, many of the promoters losing a considerable sum of money. Charles Howarth, James Smithies, William Co-oper, and James Daly, who were blessed with buoyant spirits, could not be frightened from the path by such gloomy forebodings, and Charles Howarth continually pointed out that the shoal on which the first store had been wrecked was the credit system, while in their projected plan this danger was to be avoided by supplying goods for ready money only. Night after night the undertaking was considered, and even on Sabbath afternoons they sat round the cosy fireplace of Mr. Smithies' dwelling, and pondered over the poverty of the present and the hopes of the future. They knew that hundreds in their midst were steeped in misery; that the wealthy class, who found them poor, would keep them so; that "blessed was he that considereth the poor;" and it was their ambition to devise some method to remedy the mournful state of domestic life. Although their means were small, their views were of a colossal description . . .

At length they decided to put their plans into practice as an experiment, for practical knowledge is much superior to theoretical, and to this end they bought a bag of meal at a wholesale warehouse, and divided it amongst themselves at cost price. By this means they procured this wholesome article of food at a very reduced price, and were tempted to buy a sack of potatoes, which was shared out in a like manner, and they were much benefited.

George Jacob Holyoake, a leading Owenite, reformist voice, and writer, had spoken about the issues of the day at a meeting in Rochdale in 1843. Later, Holyoake would become the leading chronicler of the success of the Rochdale Pioneers and cooperation in Britain and would travel throughout Europe and the United States actively promoting cooperatives.

The co-op held its first official meeting on Sunday, August 11, 1844. There were nine people in attendance. Elected as President was Miles Ashworth; Secretary, James Daly; and Treasurer, John Holt. The others present included

James Bamford, Charles Howarth, James Holt, James Smithies, William Taylor, and James Tweedale. At the next quarterly meeting, Charles Howarth was elected President.

The cooperators held a second meeting on August 15, at the Social Institution. On that date they adopted the motion, "That the society date its establishment, 15th August, 1844." The co-op was registered as the Rochdale Equitable Pioneers Society on October 24, 1844. It was registered under the Friendly Society Act of 1836, which limited transactions to members. It is believed that the word cooperative was purposefully left out of the name because of the negative association with the failure of the previous co-op on Toad Lane.

James Daly did not object to the use of the word "Pioneers" but he was amused by it claims Robertson, ". . . for he had in his mind's eye the pioneers who were sent forth to facilitate the progress of an army, and he remarked that they might as well call themselves 'Equitable Shovellers.' "

At this time there were no laws in England which suited the needs of the new cooperative. James Standring had obtained a copy of the Friendly Societies Act and was studying how to form an association. The by-laws eventually were fashioned after those of the Rational, Sick, and Burial Society, an insurance society established by the Owenite Manchester Congress of 1837. They were also similar to the model rules of the 1832 Congress. The founders' plan contained many of the ideas laid out by Dr. King in *The Co-operator.* The later Industrial and Provident Acts of 1853, 1862, and 1876 were all created to provide a home for the growing cooperative sector, and they allowed co-ops to sell to non-members.

Although there are a number of differing lists of the original members, most co-op historians seem willing to accept those of G. D. H. Cole, in his book *Century of Co-operation,* clarified by co-op historian Arnold Bonner in *British Co-operation.* Cole's comprehensive survey shows the twenty-eight names regarded as the original members. They were all male; their average age at the time of the founding of Rochdale was 35, and the average age at death for the twenty-eight was 64.8 years old. However, in 1844 the ages of the four key figures were as follows: Howarth (32), Smithies

(25), Ashworth (19) and Cooper (24); the average age when the store opened was 25 and at their death was 49. (See Appendix A).

The ground floor of 31 Toad Lane was for rent—the Methodists operated a day school on the middle floor, and the Bethel Chapel occupied the top floor. The three-year lease for the ground floor of Dr. Walter Dunlap's warehouse was ten pounds per year, with the first three months to be paid in advance. Dunlop, a local medical doctor who was appalled at the poverty of the working-class cooperators, would not lease to the Pioneers. Charles Howarth stepped forward, personally guaranteed the lease, and paid the first quarter's rent. The first store measured 23 feet wide and 50 feet deep, about 1150 square feet. The retail part of the store measured 23 feet wide and 17 feet deep, measuring 391 square feet. The rear section was used for inventory and meetings.

Built around 1790, the building had been used for many years as a storehouse by the Pioneer Regiment, although there is supposedly no connection with the regiment's name and that of the co-op. Many groups used the word *pioneer* in that era to suggest their position at the forefront of change. A military barracks had stood at the corner near the co-op at Toad Lane and Blackwater Street ever since the riots of 1831; the troops finally left Rochdale in 1846.

Building Capital

The weavers of Rochdale who founded modern cooperative enterprise balanced independence with interdependence, self interest with good will, and action with foresight.
—President Franklin D. Roosevelt
Greetings to Rochdale, 1944

Prior to opening the store, the Pioneers collected twenty-eight pounds in capital, one pound each from many of the twenty-eight founders at the rate of two pennies a week. William Mallalieu added one pound to his installment, and David Brooks lent the Co-op five pounds and another five pounds came from the Weavers Union. Although not all of the Pioneers were weavers, most of them were involved with either the cotton or wool weaving industry in Rochdale. Because of the level of artisanship and the age of many of the Pioneers, they became known affectionately as the Ow'd Weighvers, Lancashire dialect for old weavers.

Initially, a number of collectors, including James Tweedale and William Williams, were appointed to go from house to house on Sunday mornings to collect the members' weekly subscriptions of two or three pennies. The money was handed to the committee, which met every Sunday afternoon at James Smithies' house on Lord Street. Each member invested the equivalent of two weeks' wages and committed to a total investment of ten weeks wages. Measure that against the average investment of members in consumer cooperatives today! Does anyone today have the equivalent of ten weeks' wages as an investment in their co-op? It was this commitment of capital that gave the co-ops the resources to build their movement.

The 1854 Almanac of the Pioneers stated, "How many stores have languished for years, flabby in pocket and lean in limb because its shabby minded members starved it by hardly subscribing one pound each." The Pioneers had planned too long to want to repeat the mistakes of other co-ops who undercapitalized the business. The Pioneers were intent on listening to Dr. King's admonition: "Workmen united together must be independent. Let them save, and save, and save, to form a common capital. Let this capital be their master."

To become a member of the Rochdale Equitable Pioneers Society, individuals had to appear at a meeting, pay one shilling (twelve pennies) immediately, and commit to paying a minimum of three pennies per week or thirty-nine pennies quarterly until each member had capital equal to five pounds (five shares at one pound each) invested in the co-op. A member could not invest more than one hundred pounds, a most unlikely occurrence, since in that day one hundred pounds could buy two houses. From 1844 to 1862 the liability of members for the debts of the society was unlimited. If the co-op failed, everyone was responsible for its total debts. Any member not being able to pay regularly (except for sickness, distress, or unemployment) was fined three pennies. The co-op stated, "The amount of capital each member ought to supply in order that the store may do well for him is eight pounds."

A Financial Return Based Upon Economic Use

The concept of paying a dividend on purchases or usage is a practice which distinguishes co-ops from other enterprises. For the first hundred years of the Rochdale co-op, the dividend was both a cash machine and an equity builder. Copied all over the world, it continues to be an important member benefit bringing critical value to the cooperative. Howarth deserves immense credit for transforming the concept into reality. However, there is the possibility that Howarth first learned of the idea from Archibald Campbell. Campbell was an active Owenite, involved in the Scottish Owenite colony at Orbiston, and was one of the early organizers of the Scottish cooperative movement. Campbell had first advocated the idea of a dividend to customers rather than investors in 1830, and he lectured in Rochdale about co-ops a number of times between 1839 and 1843.

From the surplus or profits, invested member capital would receive 3.5 percent—soon increased to 5 percent—interest to attract capital. After paying interest on member capital, the store paid a quarterly dividend on purchases to the members. All interest and dividends were paid into the members' share accounts until they reached four pounds. After that, members received the interest and dividends directly in cash. The co-op developed a unique model to repay customers on the basis of upon their transactions with the society. The co-op focused reward on use and the co-op model was born.

Chapter 6

The Pioneers Make Progress

*For my own part, I am not ashamed to say that if ten years
ago anybody had prophesied to me the success of the cooperative system, as illustrated in the towns of the North, if I had
been told that laboring men would associate together for
mutual advantage, I should have regarded the prediction as
absurd. There is, in my opinion, no greater social marvel
than the manner in which these societies flourish, combined
with a consideration of the soundness of the basis on which
they are built.*
—Prime Minister William Gladstone
House of Commons, 1864

Initially, the store did from four to seven pounds in weekly
volume. Within a few months of opening, the committee
decided to expand hours and stay open every evening except
Tuesday and Sunday. They also decided to sell tea and tobacco, for which they needed licenses, so the members agreed
to raise the necessary money. Once again, as he had done
with rental of the store, Charles Howarth stepped forward to
hold the license and liability in his name. By December of
1845, the store's weekly volume was doing upwards of thirty
pounds per week.

In 1847, sales of thirty-six pounds a week were compa-
rable to those of other small shops, but five to ten times
smaller than those of larger ones. The co-op therefore did not
yet pose a challenge to the other retailers of Rochdale. Their

decision to sell at market prices meant they were not trying to use price to build their market share. The co-op had two maxims: "To be safe we must sell at a profit," and "To be honest we must sell at a profit." This focus and drive for a profitable operation was a legacy of the previous failed co-op in Rochdale. It was indeed a major reason for their defining the modern model of cooperative development. It is their economic success and growth that made the world copy the practices of the Pioneers.

At the end of the first quarter of operations, the co-op paid a dividend of three pennies per pound spent (240 pennies in a pound). The fourth quarter returned a dividend of seven pennies. Soon the co-op's dividend varied between twenty-four to thirty pennies per pound spent, or a minimum of a ten percent dividend on purchases.

The years of 1846 to 1848 were marked by slow progress and a number of setbacks. The year 1847 was a disastrous one for the economy of Britain, and there was a major cholera epidemic. The co-op also seemed to go through the same dissension of any new democratic organization, with arguments about religion and nonreligious Sunday activities at the store. A number of members withdrew. Somehow things held together, and the co-op toiled on.

Interestingly, in the midst of these setbacks, the failure of the Rochdale Savings Bank in 1849 gave the young co-op society its initial economic credibility. Most working-class people in Rochdale had deposited their meager savings in the bank, including 191 sick clubs serving 10,000 members. Disastrously, the bank's owner had used the deposits to cover losses incurred in his other industrial activities. In comparison the co-op was an attractive and solid place to invest one's hard-earned pennies. Members were also impressed that they were allowed to inspect the open books of the penny capitalists at the co-op's quarterly meetings and democratically elect the board..

In 1851, the co-op decided to open all day and they appointed the first salaried officer, James Smithies, to act as secretary. He was paid fifteen pounds per year, and was to manage a superintendent (William Cooper) and two shopmen (John Rudman and James Standring) at the weekly wages of 18, 16, and 15 shillings. All four were members of the original twenty-eight. At the same meeting, they clarified that no board member of the Pioneers shall be an employee or vice-versa.

The decade of the 1850s was one of tremendous growth for the Pioneers. At the end of 1850 there were 390 members and a retail volume of 13,179 pounds. In 1860 there were 3,450 members and a retail volume of 152,063 pounds, approximately a tenfold increase. The Pioneers' growth and profitability allowed them to pursue many different opportunities.

Members from the Castleton district of Rochdale petitioned the board in 1856 to open a store on their side of town, and within three months the first branch store was open. A smaller cooperative society asked to be merged with the Pioneers, and their store became the second branch store on March 7, 1857. Members in different parts of Rochdale immediately petitioned for a store in their neighborhood, and the Pioneers opened two other branches by June 2, 1857. By 1860 there were eight branches, and by 1875 there were sixteen. Ten out of the sixteen stores were owned by the co-op, and twelve of the sixteen had newsrooms.

The co-op began with a grocery department in 1844, added a butchers' department in 1846, then a drapery department in 1847, and later added shoemaking in 1852. In 1855 the Pioneers opened a wholesale department from which they made their joint buying available to other societies. By 1856 the Pioneers had also opened up another shop at 8 Toad Lane, probably to display and manufacture shoes and tailoring. A little later the Pioneers opened a furnishings showroom across the road from 31 Toad. Other services were added such as bakeries, dairies, building and painting, laundry, and coal delivery. Many of these were all brought together when the Central Stores were opened in 1867.

As the Pioneers were then linked with the Christian Socialists and other progressive groups (the Red), a number of other co-ops were founded. The Conservative Industrial Society (the Blue) was started, then an Irish Society (the Green) began, and later the Rochdale Provident (the Yellow), a group that did not like the links with the Cooperative Wholesale

Society. By 1874 the Pioneers had 6,444 members, the Conservatives had 1,206, and the Provident had 884. The Green had already died, the Blue would be next, and the Yellow merged with the Pioneers in 1933.

From the very start, the Pioneers had been concerned about the adulteration of food. In a protest against the adulteration of flour by the local millers, the Pioneers decided to start the Rochdale District Cooperative Corn Mill Society in 1850. The mill grew so fast that a new mill was erected in 1856, and by 1862 the new mill was supplying fifty-six co-op stores. The mill was enlarged three times, and when the Cooperative Congress met in Rochdale in 1892 the mill employed over seventy people. However, with the changes in transportation and national competition, the local co-ops generally agreed to turn over the milling business to the Cooperative Wholesale Society milling division.

Another business owing its start to the Pioneers was the Rochdale Cooperative Manufacturing Society. This society was a cooperative partnership of capital and labor. The Society had the support of many cooperators anxious to see labor gain a return on their efforts in partnership with capital. Many of the mill workers and partners had seen the fruits of cooperation through the growth of their shares in the Pioneers Society and the Corn Mill. Because of its cooperative nature, the Mitchell Hey Mill was the last to lay off people during the Cotton Famine and the first to take everyone back. However, at the end of the famine, with speculation in the air, the society stopped sharing profits with the workers to increase the profits paid to capital. From that day on, the mill lost its cooperative flavor and became a normal joint stock company.

As the Pioneers made progress, a coherent philosophy emerged. The cooperative idea was born in a revolutionary era, but the dour Pioneers mounted a unique "counter-revolution." When members exchanged money over the counter for the cooperative's goods, an empire was born, an empire meant to equalize, not to exploit. The Pioneers believed that trading together could build a better world, one without conflict. Revolutions were occurring frequently throughout Europe, and groups secretly plotted to overthrow governments.

While others urged armed revolt, strikes, and mass action on the streets, the cooperators quietly built the people's business. Amidst the revolutionary working-class fervor, cooperators adopted "Labor and Wait" as a motto, the beehive as a symbol to suggest industriousness, and solid brand names such as "Perseverance," "Federation," and "Anchor."

Chapter 7

Champions of the Co-op

Pride Builds an Idea

O Teacher of Teachers and Helper of all,
Thou knowest our need, and thou hearest our call —
Give strength to they servants their task to fulfill,
And send forth, we pray thee, more labourers still.

(This hymn was sung at the Unitarian Chapel, Clover Street,
Rochdale on Sunday, October 20, 1844, four days before the co-op
was incorporated. A number of the Pioneers were chapel members.)

Most of the original members of the Pioneers had been active or sympathetic to the Chartist cause. Many had also been followers of Robert Owen. After Chartism ebbed, a large portion of the Pioneers would describe themselves as socialists. Yet at the same time many of them were very religious and participated in the growth of the nondenominational church and chapel movement. The birth of religious movements outside of the established Church of England was another attempt to wrest power away from existing institutions. The co-op and the chapel walked hand in hand down the road to a more democratic land. More importantly, as is often the case in history, existing groups gave birth and support to new groups. Three groups stand out in particular as providing an early home for discussions, membership re cruitment, and organizing support for the co-op.

The Unitarians

The Unitarian Chapel on Clover Street, built in 1818, became known as the "Co-op Chapel." A number of Unitarians
played important roles in developing the co-op: Miles
Ashworth became the first President (he was one of the
guards sent to accompany Napoleon when exiled to the is-
land of St. Helena in 1818); his son, Samuel Ashworth, one of
the first shopkeepers; James Smithies, the chief of the fight-
ing Pioneers and the only one to become a member of the
Rochdale Town Council; and James Wilkinson, a lay pastor
at the Chapel for forty years, who gave the hard-working
members a home on Sunday. Charles Howarth became a
leader in the nearby Heywood Unitarian Church.

The Socialists' Institute

The other institution supportive of the Pioneers in its
early days was the Socialists' Institute, founded in 1838 next
door to the Weavers Arms. Thomas Livesy, later an Alderman
of Rochdale and a good friend of the Pioneers, was the treasurer of the Institute. The Institute sponsored fervent debates among the Chartists, Owenites, and socialists. One
minute they were foes at the Institute, the next minute they
were friends at the Weavers' Arms. The proximity of the two
was good for politics. The "pubs and clubs" of the North were
the centers of working-class life. Here, the ideas of the day
were discussed, and various friendly societies were organized
and operated. Even the teetotalers had their temperance
halls. Working people might be willing to go without a drink,
but they were not willing to go without their pub. It was in
the pub, club, and chapel that the early Pioneers would
gather with their friends and supporters and gain the confidence to meet the challenges of another day.

Christian Socialists

In the early days of the co-op's existence, the Christian
Socialists became their legal and parliamentary champions.
The Christian Socialists were influenced by Frederick
Denison Maurice, who wrote *The Kingdom of Christ*. The au-

thor identified a progressive social message within the teachings of Christ, and that message was taken up by a group of respectable and learned followers. One of the first was Charles Kingsley, author of *Alton Locke*. Kingsley wrote to Maurice in the summer of 1844 asking for a meeting with Maurice to gain his advice on how to be an activist Christian.

Other leading Christian Socialists included Thomas Hughes, author of *Tom Brown's School Days*, John Malcolm Ludlow, a famous lawyer of the day, and Edward Vansittart Neale. For many years, the Christian Socialists gave lectures in the halls of the local cooperatives throughout Britain. Often, they were keynote speakers at the Cooperative Congress and would come to Rochdale to teach in the classes given by the Pioneers. Quite a few Christian Socialists wrote widely read pamphlets on cooperation. Many of them were also strong internationalists and played an important role in fostering the beginnings of the International Cooperative Alliance.

Educated at Oxford and later a renowned barrister, Neale was to give his professional life and most of his sizable family fortune to building the cooperative movement. Neale drafted the Industrial and Provident Societies Act of 1852, which gave birth to the freedom of cooperative trade. The Act removed the numerous restrictions placed upon cooperatives, particularly those that limited co-ops from working together on joint ventures, the ownership of property, and the raising of capital. This act is known as the "Magna Charta of Co-operation."

Later, in 1876, Neale played the key role in drafting amendments to the Industrial and Provident Societies Act, which allowed the single retail cooperatives to branch out or to federate into wholesaling, banking, and distribution. Neale also played a major role in drafting the incorporation papers of the Co-operative Wholesale Society, the Co-operative Insurance Company, the Co-operative Newspaper Society, the Co-operative Production Federation, and the Co-operative Union.

Roy Garratt, the Curator of the Pioneers Museum and the Librarian of the Cooperative Union, calls Neale "the unknown giant of Co-operation" for all he accomplished on behalf of the movement. Neale worked ceaselessly for development of worker cooperatives and for profit sharing with workers in consumer cooperatives. Garratt recounts, "Altogether in the 1850s Neale spent some 40,000 pounds of his own money (about 2 million pounds in today's money) on these cooperatives."

Neale died in 1892, having seen the co-op movement grow from one store to thousands and the idea spread all across the world. His steady role in guiding critical legislation through Parliament should be regarded as the passport to progress for the cooperative movement. At death, he was honored both by cooperators and by the nation. A memorial service was held for him at St. Paul's Cathedral in London, where a permanent plaque was unveiled in the crypt. The inscription reads:

He neither power nor riches sought.
For others, not himself, he fought.
Union is strength.

His contribution to cooperatives should never be forgotten.

South East Lancashire Folk — Proud People

Historically, Toad Lane was one of the busiest streets, leading directly to the open-air market and town center of Rochdale. There is a belief that its original name was "The Old Lane" which was changed by Lancashire dialect into T'owd Lane. An 1831 map shows Toad Lane as being the original road from northern Lancashire into the center of Rochdale. On the map, Toad Lane is depicted as "old road to Whitworth," further reason to believe that T'owd Lane has veracity.

John Collier, creator of the character "Tim Bobbin," Samuel Bamford, and Edwin Waugh are the three greatest writers of Lancashire dialect. They all had strong ties to Rochdale and co-ops and were builders of regional working-class pride. John Collier's son, Tom, addressed a crowd of thirteen thousand at Rochdale a fortnight before Peterloo, and Tom's nephew, John, became one of the earnest original

Pioneers. John Collier even had the early co-op symbol, the beehive, carved on his grave.

Edwin Waugh (1817-1890), the famous Lancashire dialect writer, was born in Rochdale, near "Old Clock Face" on Toad Lane. In 1844, Waugh returned from London to Rochdale and must have observed the new co-op. Waugh was the author of the first song published in Lancashire dialect, which appeared in *The Manchester Examiner* in 1856. Waugh was an honored speaker at many co-op meetings and at the opening of the Milkstone co-op store of the Pioneers Society in 1872. It was from the Milkstone store in Rochdale during the Second World War that the BBC broadcast the greetings from Rochdale to cooperators in the United States in 1944.

Waugh used the appetite of the newspaper age to spread the virtues of Lancashire dialect to a growing working-class readership. The rise of Manchester as "Cotton Capital of the World" led to a growth in regional pride. The opening of the Manchester Royal Exchange in 1874 and the 36-mile-long Manchester Ship Canal opened in 1894 were the two most physical proofs that Manchester was emerging as the second most important city of England, after London. The unique northern dialect was now a part of the robust Industrial Revolution, but not always welcome in the drawing rooms of London. That bias drove people in the North to see themselves as different from people in the South.

Samuel Bamford, who worked in London over a decade, said, "I have heard more common sense spoken in half an hour in a Lancashire tap room than I heard in my whole stay in London." The way was paved for the arrival of the protest novel written in dialect. In 1848, a transplanted southerner, Elizabeth Gaskell, published *Mary Barton*, a story about life in Manchester during the Chartist era. It was the first national best-seller to feature Lancashire dialect.

Writing in his preface to *Lancashire Sketches*, published in 1881, Waugh wrote, "Lancashire has some learned writers who have written upon themes generally and locally interesting... but for native force and truth John Collier and Samuel Bamford are probably the foremost of all genuine expositors of the characteristics of the Lancashire people."

Through their work, the three writers each gave the ordinary people of Lancashire the self-esteem needed to perform extraordinary acts. Flush with the immense changes occurring in society, working people were no longer passive. The co-ops were beneficiaries of this pride as Lancashire people stood together to build a strong and expansive movement. The dialect writers elevated the rich qualities of working people and added color to the culture of South Lancashire. With their newly found pride, working people were prepared to take on the impossible. To commemorate Rochdale's role in dialect writing, the town was chosen as the site for the Lancashire Dialect Writers' Memorial.

Chapter 8

Co-op— The Pioneer of Pure Food

*The energetic and enterprising pursuit of such policies, often
in the face of a hostile public, is a striking testimony to the
faith of the early co-operators. Through them, and through
them alone, some at least of the working-classes were famil-
iarized with a standard of purity they had never before
known, and were educated to an appreciation of the moral as
well as the economic value of honest dealing.*
— John Burnett
Plenty and Want

Newspaper reports and studies of the 1840s show that
sugar and rice cost twelve pennies per pound, pure milk
was too expensive for any working person to buy, and the
milk they tried to sell to working people was too watered
down to be worth it. Most working people drank concoctions
of dried apple leaves, because the cheapest sort of real tea
was ninety-six pennies per pound. Beer ranged from twelve
to eighteen pennies per gallon, and was drunk all too often in
place of tea. Only a few families ate meat more than once a
week, usually in a stew, and many could afford it only for
Christmas. Few people ate fruit unless it was stolen. Arrests
for stealing from orchards were usually highest on Sundays,
the one day off for working people. Bread was ten pennies a
loaf. Only potatoes were cheap enough for everyone. Cab-

bages, potatoes, bread, and beer were the unappetizing diet staples of working people.

In addition to being expensive, much available food had substantial impurities. Flour was commonly adulterated with ground beans, plaster of Paris, and ground bones. Some sugar was found to be half salt. Tea was supplemented with iron filings and other minerals or chemicals. To this day, the London Cockney slang for thief is "tea leaf."

In 1844 *The Liverpool Echo* reported:

Salted butter is sold for fresh, the lumps being covered with a coating of fresh butter, or a pound of fresh being laid on top to taste, while the salted article is sold after this test, or the whole mass is washed and then sold as fresh. With sugar, pounded rice and other cheap adulterating materials are mixed, and the whole sold at full price. The refuse of soap-boiling establishments also is mixed with other things and sold as sugar. Chicory and other cheap stuff is mixed with ground coffee, and artificial coffee beans with the unground article. Cocoa is often adulterated with fine brown earth, treated with fat to tender it more easily mistakable for real cocoa. Tea is mixed with the leaves of sloe and with other refuse, or dry tea-leaves are roasted on hot copper plates, so returning to the proper colour and being sold as fresh. Pepper is mixed with pounded nut-shells; port-wine is manufactured outright (out of alcohol, dye-stuffs, etc.), while it is notorious that more of it is consumed in England alone than is grown in Portugal; and tobacco is mixed with disgusting substances of all sorts and in all possible forms in which the article is produced.

Engels also shared his observations on life around Manchester in 1844:

But the poor, the working people, to whom a couple of farthings are important, who must buy many things with little money, who cannot afford to inquire too closely into the quality of their purchases, and cannot do so in any case because they have had no opportunity of cultivating their taste—to their share fall all the adulterated, poisoned provisions. They must deal with the small retailers, must buy perhaps on credit, and these small retail dealers who cannot sell even the same quality of goods so cheaply as the largest retailers, because of their small capital and the large proportional expenses of their business, must knowingly or unknowingly buy adulterated goods in order to sell at the lower prices required, and to meet the competition of the others. . . Not in the quality alone, but in the quantity of his goods as well, is the English working man defrauded. The small dealers usually have false weights and measures, and an incredible number of convictions for such offences may be read in the police reports. How universal this form of fraud is in the manufacturing districts, a couple of extracts from *The Manchester Guardian* may serve to show. They cover only a short period, and, even here, I have not all the numbers at hand:

Guardian, 16 June 1844, Rochdale Sessions—Four dealers fined five to ten shillings for using light weights. Stockport Sessions—Two dealers fined one shilling, one of them having seven light weights and a false scale, and both having been warned.

Guardian, 19 June, Rochdale Sessions—One dealer fined five, and two farmers ten shillings.

Guardian, 22 June, Manchester Justices of the Peace—Nineteen dealers fined two shillings and sixpence to two pounds.

Guardian, 26 June, Ashton Sessions—Fourteen dealers and farmers fined two shillings and sixpence to one pound. Hyde Petty Sessions—Nine farmers and dealers condemned to pay costs and five shillings fines.

Guardian, 9 July, Manchester—Sixteen dealers condemned to pay costs and fines not exceeding ten shillings.

Guardian, 13 July, Rochdale—Nine dealers fined from two shillings and six pence to twenty shillings.

Guardian, 24 July, Rochdale—Four dealers fined ten to twenty shillings.

Provision of pure unadulterated food was an early goal of the Rochdale Pioneers. However, in 1843, Holyoake had warned them: "When you have a little store and have reached the point of getting pure provisions, you may find your purchasers will not like them, nor know them when they taste them. Their taste will require to be educated." When the co-ops entered into their own production with the Rochdale Flour Mill, their natural products were resisted by a public used to white and shiny foods. In 1852, the Cooperative Central Agency, the first national buying group, published a pamphlet to educate members about pure food and held lectures on the subject throughout the country.

Holyoake's predictions were quite accurate. The "pure food" goals of the co-op were no easy task. When they were unable to locate high-quality flour, the Rochdale and Brickfield co-ops entered into a joint venture with individuals to start a mill in 1850. Initially, the mill did poorly because the members complained that the flour was much darker than the lighter-colored adulterated flour they were used to. Fortunately, the Pioneers took Holyoake's advice and an education campaign won the day. Flour sales increased, and the mill became profitable.

In 1860, the first Food and Drugs Act was passed; however, in 1861, a lecture at the Royal Society revealed that 87 percent of the bread and 74 percent of the milk sold in London was still adulterated. It was not until the Act was amended in 1872 that the identification and suppression of food adulteration was made more effective.

The commitment to honest weight was continued by the wholesale societies. In 1882, when the Scottish and English Co-operative Wholesale Societies entered into a partnership to sell tea, they agreed that the member should get sixteen ounces of tea in the package. This practice differed from those of other grocers, who put the tea in heavy paper packaging and declared the whole package to be sixteen ounces. The Rochdale co-op practice of giving sixteen ounces to the pound became the law of the land during World War I.

The emphasis on pure food continued to be a main objective of the co-ops. In the November 4, 1871, issue of *The Co-operative News* there is an advertisement placed by the Co-operative Farming Society consisting of a prospectus for a new farm to be run on cooperative principles with shares sold at ten shillings each. The temporary offices of the society were located at the headquarters of the Co-operative Wholesale Society in Manchester. The board was composed of members from a number of different Lancashire cooperatives. "The object of this society is to raise a sufficient capital to establish a Farm in a convenient locality, within easy access of Manchester, for the purpose of supplying its members and the public with pure and unadulterated articles of farm produce."

In the same issue of *The Co-operative News* there is also an advertisement by the Agricultural and Horticultural Co-operative Association proclaiming:

> The association was formed in 1867 to supply its members with Farm, Garden and Household requisites, of ascertained purity and highest quality, as nearly as possible at wholesale prices. The Association employs an Analytical Chemist to examine all goods contracted for, and nothing but unadulterated goods of the highest quality are dealt in.

In 1874, a House of Commons Committee investigated food adulteration and reported that people were "cheated rather than poisoned." In the following year, Parliament passed the Sale of Food and Drug Act which, as W. Henry Brown wrote, "minimized the cheating and lessened the risk of poisoning. But the Rochdale Pioneers had initiated such a trading policy thirty years before. Parliament followed the Pioneers."

Chapter 9

Cotton, Co-ops, and the U.S. Civil War (1861-1865)

The Co-op Withstands the Cotton Famine

The moral miracle performed by our Co-operators at Rochdale is that they had the good sense to differ without disagreeing; to dissent with each other without separating; to hate at times, and yet always to hold together.
— **George Jacob Holyoake**

In 1861 the population of Lancashire was 2,428,440—nearly one-eighth of the population of England and Wales. One million people were employed in Lancashire's textile trade. People throughout Britain poured into the area, eager to find their fortune. The port of Liverpool, which contained 78,000 people in 1801, grew to 438,000 by 1861. The Liverpool Exchange was the center of the raw cotton trade, and Liverpool became a busier port than London. Manchester had grown from 94,000 in 1801 to 460,000 in 1861, and it was the "capital of the north." Rochdale itself had grown from 14,000 in 1801 to 68,000 in 1841.

There were 1,900 cotton mills in Lancashire in 1860. With its looms relentlessly spinning hour after hour, Lancashire was the thriving economic engine of Britain. In 1861 the cotton trade exceeded the gross revenue of the British government for the first time. Capital was receiving interest of 30 to 40 percent. Cotton was indeed king in the American South and in the English North, but its crown was about to be removed.

The early 1860s would be another testing time for the Pioneers of Rochdale. The American Civil War broke out, the North blockaded the South, and the cotton mills of Lancashire could not get their cotton from the Southern plantations in the USA. By 1861, the Confederacy was founded. Two weeks later the news reached Liverpool by cotton boat. That day the price of cotton drove up dramatically and wages for the millworkers went down drastically. On April 12, 1861, brother turned against brother in the U.S. Their blood drenched the American earth. Lancashire's industry died with them as King Cotton collapsed overnight. Of all the English counties, Lancashire bore the greatest brunt of the Civil War.

By November 1861, 49 Lancashire Mills had closed, 119 were on half-time, and eight thousand cotton mill workers were out of work. That same year, withdrawals from savings banks outpaced deposits by the largest amount since the "Hungry Forties." On August 7, 1862, eight thousand cotton operatives met on Lobden Moor to consider the distressed condition of the district. Because of the American Civil War, 8,359 people were out of work in Rochdale in 1863.

Edwin Waugh, a Rochdale native born on Toad Lane, described life during the Cotton Famine of the 1860s:

> Just previous to the mills beginning to work short time, four of their five children had been lying ill, all at once, for five months; and before that trouble befell them, one of the lads had two of his fingers taken off whilst working at the factory, and so was disabled a good while. It takes little additional weight to sink those whose chins are only just above water; and these untoward circumstances oiled the way of this struggling family to the ground before the mills stopped. A few months' want of work, with their little stock of shop stuff oozing away—partly on credit to their poor neighbours, and partly to live upon them-

selves—and they became destitute of all, except a few beggarly remnants of empty shop furniture. (Lancashire Sketches, II, 212-213)

The severity of the hunger was immense. At the end of 1862, the soup kitchen in Rochdale was feeding 18,000 people and the Guardians providing relief to 13,226 people each week. In 1863, nearly 27 percent of Rochdale's citizens were receiving relief. In response, Rochdale, always the pioneer, was the second town in Lancashire to form local relief efforts. John Bright, ever the Quaker, implored the citizens to help themselves. The Reverend Charles Kingsley, then also chaplain to Queen Victoria, joined in the national effort to raise money to send to the suffering people of Lancashire. President Abraham Lincoln was well aware of the suffering and sent the following message to the people of Manchester on January 19, 1863:

I know and deeply deplore the sufferings which the working people of Manchester and in all of Europe are called to endure in this crisis. It has been often and studiously represented that the attempt to overthrow this government which was built on the foundation of human rights, and to substitute for it one which should rest exclusively on the band of slavery was likely to obtain the favor of Europe. . . Under these circumstances I cannot but regard your decisive utterances upon the question as an instance of sublime Christian heroism which has not been surpassed in any age or in any country. It is indeed an energetic and re-inspiring assurance of the inherent truth and of the ultimate and universal triumph of justice, humanity and freedom. . . I hail the interchange of sentiments, therefore as an augury that, whatever else may happen, whatever misfortune may befall your country or my own, the peace and friendship which now exists between the two nations will be, as it shall be my desire to make them, perpetual.

Fortunately, the voters of Rochdale had returned Cobden as their M.P. in April 1859, even though he was in the United States at the time. Abraham Greenwood, a Rochdale native and a champion of the cooperative wholesale was one of Cobden's official nominees. The election had been a bitter one, with the shopkeepers attacking Cobden as well as Bright for being the champions of the Rochdale Pioneers. Cobden's voice energized the nation to help Lancashire, and he issued the challenge, "We need a million pounds." The driving force behind the Lancashire relief efforts was Rochdale-born Sir James Kay-Shuttleworth, who had been brought out of retirement for the cause.

John Bright, always full of practical ideas, made a suggestion to U.S. Senator Charles Sumner. If people in the North could organize a donation of flour to the people of Lancashire, it would make for excellent propaganda. Collections were conducted in New York, and ship owner George Griswold offered to transport the food for free. His ship docked in Liverpool in February of 1863 with fifteen thousand barrels of flour on board. For many years, John Bright displayed one of the barrels at his factory in Rochdale.

Norman Longmate's book, *The Hungry Mills*, points out that Britain's role in the American Civil War was an extremely mixed one. He argues that, in general, public opinion in Lancashire was cautiously favorable to the South. Most people looked at it as a bread-and-butter issue—they wanted work but were not favorable to slavery.

"Only one cotton town stood out against the prevailing tide, the town where John Bright had both his business and his home," Longmate reports.

"It was a great time in Rochdale," wrote Bright's daughter, "with all its cotton workers in idleness and . . . alive to the reason. A meeting was called in the town in 1863 by a Liverpool association of Southern sympathies, formed to promote the breaking up of the blockade. The lecturer delivered his address, and the meeting passed a resolution censuring him for endeavoring to mislead them."

Supporters of the Northern Program ultimately took control of the hall and severely mishandled the lecturer.

Jacob Bright had moved to Rochdale in 1802 and started the second cotton mill in the town. When Lord Byron sold the manorial rights to the Dearden family, municipal affairs fell into neglect. Parliament had to appoint Commissioners to take responsibility for the town. Jacob Bright, then the local leader of the Quakers, worked hard to deal with the town's problems. Rochdale's leading citizens petitioned Parliament for a Municipal Charter. When it was awarded a charter in 1856, Jacob Bright became the first mayor. As Mayor, Jacob Bright agreed to be one of the Arbitrators for the Cooperative Manufacturing Society and the Corn Mill Society.

Jacob's son would become one of the nineteenth century's most remembered politicians. John Bright (1811-1889) was a radical Quaker orator and "Free Trader" who developed a thriving cotton manufacturing business in Rochdale with his father and his brothers. John Bright was one of the keynote speakers at the opening of the new Free Trade Hall in Manchester in 1843. The Free Trade Hall in Manchester was built on the Peterloo site. That year John Bright was elected M.P. for Durham. By 1847, the Brights employed one thousand people in Rochdale. In 1868, John Bright was received by Queen Victoria when he became President of the Board of Trade. He was the first Quaker to become a Minister of the Crown yet he never forgot the yearning for democracy and the example set by the Pioneers.

> Mr. John Bright, when speaking in the House of Commons on the 18th of June, 1860, on the subject of Parliamentary Reform, dwelt on the history of the Rochdale Pioneers' Society, the Corn Mill Society, and the Manufacturing Society; and in passing a high eulogium on the members of these societies, said: "I have thought it desirable to place these facts before the House because I am able to produce evidence of everything I have said in regard to them, for I know many of these men and the establishments. I know something of the working population among whom I live, and I believe there is not a person in this House who will dare to stand up after I sit down, and

say with respect to the men who have thus conducted a large business, saved their money, and promoted all these means of spreading education, intelligence, and sobriety amongst the people, that it would be perilous to the institutions of this country—if those institutions are worth anything—to give such men a vote for members of Parliament."

Soon the tide would turn in America against slavery but freedom would come a century later.

On April 9, 1865, General Robert E. Lee surrendered at Appomattox, Virginia, and the dreams of the Confederacy died. At the time Rochdale was full of electioneering for the seat previously held by Richard Cobden. On election night, poll results were being announced every hour in the town square, where a crowd began to build that soon filled the square. The final result: Thomas Bayley Potter had been elected to succeed Cobden. Speaking to the great gathering, Potter thanked the people and then paused, "But I have better news for you. Richmond has fallen." A. Henry Brown wrote, "Then arose a cheer more deafening than any of the previous shoutings . . ." The son of the American Minister at Paris had gone to Rochdale to witness an English election and was standing with Potter. He remarked, "Mr. Potter, if that cheer could have been carried across the Atlantic, Americans would think very differently of your country."

Bright admired Abraham Lincoln and strongly supported the North during the U.S. Civil War. His greatest service to his country was in keeping Britain out of the war on the side of the South. Because of the role of John Bright and the support of Rochdale for the North during the Civil War, the United States government presented Rochdale Town Hall with a bound volume of the addresses to Mrs. Lincoln after President Lincoln's assassination. In 1865 there had been a Town Hall meeting to express indignation at the assassination of President Lincoln. In 1871, the American Consul presented President Lincoln's gold-headed staff to John Bright, in accordance with the President's wishes.

On November 16, 1881, John Bright's seventieth birthday was celebrated by Rochdale's citizenry. There was a torchlight procession to Cronkeyshaw, where thirty thousand people joined in the festivities. When Bright died in 1889, the people of Rochdale gave him the biggest funeral of the century. Bright had been at different times an M.P. for Rochdale, Manchester, and Birmingham during the era of reform. His leadership on the issues of the day and his strong sympathies for the needs of working people made him one of the true heroes of his age. At Birmingham on January 20, 1864, John Bright had said:

> My clients have not been generally, the rich and the great, but rather the poor and the lowly. They cannot give me place of honor and dignity and wealth: but honorable service in their cause yields me that which is of higher and more lasting value.

The British labor historian Asa Briggs described Bright as one of the most militant and eloquent middle-class radical politicians of his time, whose tactics as much as his principles were frequently criticized.

Rochdale was suffering badly as a result of the American Civil War. The cotton industry almost came to a standstill, and Lancashire verged on economic ruin. In 1862 the soup kitchens at Rochdale were feeding eighteen thousand people per week and the Poor Guardians were assisting thirteen thousand people a week. In 1863 there were over eight thousand people unemployed in Rochdale, mostly as a result of the Civil War.

William Cooper later reflected on the meaning of the American Civil War to the co-op:

> Though the people have been great sufferers by the struggle brought on by the slaveholders in America none of the unprincipled advocates of the abominable cause of the South could move them from siding with the North and freedom of the slave; for the people love liberty and would not help to hold another people in bondage.

Lord Brougham spoke to the National Association of Social Science in 1863 about how the force of the Pioneers' newsroom and education program shielded their cooperative from the ravages of the Cotton Famine. He concluded his remarks by stating that the Pioneers were "a striking example of the beneficial influence of Cooperation."

There is one postscript to this part of the story. During the Cotton Famine, the Union and Emancipation Society of Manchester was key in affecting public opinion. Its president was Thomas Bayley Potter, M.P. for Rochdale. J. C. Edwards and E. O. Greening, both ardent cooperators, were the honorable secretaries. Edwards was cashier for the Co-operative Wholesale Society from its start and remained in that position until 1868. Brown tells the story of Edwards' enthusiastic and unflagging support of the American cause. When the Co-operative Wholesale Society adopted its distinctive motto, "Labour and Wait," Edwards suggested that it should rather adopt "Labor and Wait," to permanently remind cooperators of the role of freedom and to honor the American cause. The change delighted the Co-operative Wholesale Society board, many of whom came from Rochdale and nearby towns.

With Thomas Bayley Potter, M. P., in the chair, the Union Society held its final meeting on January 22, 1866. Mr. Goldwin Smith, the society's secretary, ended his farewell address with these words: "Slavery is dead everywhere and forever." Within hours, he was in the co-op at Toad Lane celebrating with friends and cooperators and signing the visitors' book. Smith reminded the gathered cooperators to be watchful of all things essential to human well-being. John Bright came into the store shortly afterward and added his to the other honored names in the Toad Lane visitors' book.

The war was over, and worries about the price of raw cotton were once again the talk of Liverpool. From a height of over 485,000 people on relief in December of 1862, the numbers dropped dramatically, and by May of 1865 the count stood at 76,000. Lancashire had weathered the storm, but not without cost. Cotton was no longer king. Manchester and Liverpool had adapted to the war by weaning themselves away from a heavy reliance on cotton. That same April of 1865, Richard Cobden died. On the day of his funeral all the shops and the eight branches of the Society were closed for three hours as a mark of respect for everything Cobden had done for the co-op and for Rochdale. Knowing slavery had been defeated and Rochdale revived, Cobden was at peace with the world he had changed.

Two events in the late 1860s mark the successful evolution of the co-op and the town of Rochdale through the Civil War years. As an M.P. in 1866, Bright laid the foundation stone for the Rochdale Town Hall, with all the co-op leaders in attendance. Opened in 1871, the Town Hall is one of the finest neo-Gothic buildings in England and is a lavish Victorian tribute to the creation of individual wealth and the newly arrived mill owners. It stands as one of the most exquisite representatives of Victorian architecture in Britain, 303 feet long and ornately decorated. The Town Hall dwarfed every other municipal building in the region with its magnificent spire rising 240 feet into the sky. A later fire destroyed the spire, and a clock tower similar to Big Ben was built in its place. The Great Hall in the Rochdale Town Hall is now the site of most major events in Rochdale. The Great Hall will be the venue for a ceremonial dinner on December 21, 1994, as the concluding event of the 150th anniversary celebrations.

Just minutes away lay the new Central Stores of the Pioneers, a thriving tribute to the practices and principles of mutual self-help. It was a proud day for the seven thousand members when the Pioneers' Central Stores opened on September 28, 1867. The Mayor of Rochdale, Mr. J. Robinson, presided over the ceremonies, and co-op supporters Thomas Hughes, M.P., E. V. Neale, George Jacob Holyoake, and E. O. Greening were among the speakers. An invited speaker and special guest at the Co-op's opening ceremonies was a Colonel Hinton from Washington, D. C. Colonel Hinton had trained and commanded Black regiments to fight for their freedom on the side of the North during the Civil War.

The four-story Central Stores building was topped by an attractive beehive adorned by a large clock. For years, the beehive had been a symbol of hard work and cooperation. A beehive now decorates the rear wall of the Pioneers Museum on Toad Lane. On the fourth floor, at the top of the central stores building, was the Pioneers' Hall, which could hold 1,500 people. The co-op included a huge newsroom to house the newspapers and magazines of the day. In the tradition of the Pioneers, the massive department store, built at a cost of 13,400 pounds cost much less than the 155,000 pounds it cost to build the Town Hall. The Pioneers' new store paid for itself quickly. The Pioneers did not mind a big building as long as it made "brass" (money in Lancashire dialect).

The new stores stood at the juncture of St. Mary's Gate and Toad Lane, at the site of the former Weslayan Chapel, then the Old Theatre (built in 1793). How much of Rochdale's past had taken place at that site: the simple preaching of the founder of Methodism, John Wesley; the Chartist rousings of the Irish orator, Feargus O' Connor; the public passion of the popular local M.P., Richard Cobden; and the pacifism and pragmatism of John Bright, the Quaker mill owner, M.P., and Minister of the Crown. The Pioneers were keeping good company.

Chapter 10

Together They Build

Co-operation Among Co-operatives

They took their affairs into their own hands, and what is
more to the purpose they kept them in their own hands.
—*George Jacob Holyoake*

Rochdale's success was being repeated across Britain.
Within two decades of Rochdale's founding there were
hundreds of co-ops to be found in almost every major city and
in many villages of northern England. The Rochdale principles and practices were being ardently followed and the
flourishing dividend copied. Cooperative missionaries were
in demand, speakers were rushing from one meeting to another, and the cooperative idea was the talk of the town. As
the co-ops grew in neighboring towns they recognized there
were many opportunities to unite together to increase their
business and reduce their costs. Like bricklayers, they knew
that placing one brick on top of the other was the surest way
to build a foundation for the cooperative movement.

On August 12, 1860, a meeting was called that would
change the face of cooperation forever. From that meeting
emerged the impetus for the Co-operative Wholesale Society,
followed by the Co-operative Insurance Society and, later, the
Co-operative Union. Attending the meeting were representatives of cooperatives from Rochdale, Oldham, Manchester,
and other towns of east Lancashire. They were meeting to

discuss formation of a jointly owned cotton mill, but reports of the meeting show that the topic which galvanized the attendees was, once again, discussion of a developing wholesale cooperative.

Time and time again the creation of a wholesale business occupied cooperators' discussions. It came up at conferences, was often written about in articles, and was the conversation of managers and the goal of numerous boards of directors. The continuing growth of existing cooperative societies and the development of new ones heightened the need. Rochdale had even attempted a wholesale agency, which it had to finally close down.

The meeting took place at Jumbo Farm near Middleton, six miles from Rochdale. The farm was a favorite meeting place for the area cooperators. Its central location made it easy for cooperators from a number of major societies to meet there on weekends. The atmosphere of the farm was also conducive to the dreams of cooperators. It was established in 1851 when a group of cottage workers decided to go back to the land. They rented the farm and six acres and renamed it Lowbands, in honor of the Chartist Estate in Gloucestershire. When they ran into economic trouble, they hired George Booth as manager. He helped them form the Jumbo Co-operative Society and opened up a small neighborhood co-op store at the farm. By 1861, the members sold off their assets and merged into the nearby Middleton Society. Booth was later appointed as an official of the Co-operative Wholesale Society .

For a decade Jumbo Farm was host to gatherings of numerous cooperative, labor, and other progressive groups. Its open-air atmosphere provided an attractive place for teas, picnics, and Sunday festivals. In that era, a day in the country on a farm was a cherished opportunity for working people. With Sunday being the only day off for most people, a picnic at Jumbo Farm was an eagerly anticipated activity.

Since 1856, George Booth had been an active supporter of the idea of a cooperative wholesale business. As host of the 1860 gathering at Jumbo Farm, he introduced the topic of the Wholesale Society. The talk ran again to the problems of starting a cooperative wholesale business, due to the limitations of the law, which prevented cooperatives from investing in other corporations. At that time, there was no mechanism for primary cooperatives to organize secondary cooperatives such as wholesales. They could start a joint stock company or assign ownership to individuals to hold in trust, but there was great caution against either method. Once again those assembled adjourned without an answer.

After further meetings at Jumbo Farm and elsewhere in the area, the group drew up a five-point platform of legal rights:

◆ Cooperatives to be allowed to own more than one acre of land
◆ Acquisition of property to be unrestricted
◆ Cooperatives to be allowed to invest in other societies or companies
◆ Limited liability to be given under the Industrial and Provident Acts
◆ Educational grants to be given legality

This platform was reported to a conference of fifty to sixty delegates held on Christmas Day in 1860, under a railway arch in Manchester. The committee that drew up the platform included Charles Howarth, "the constitution maker" of the Rochdale Pioneers, and two of the twenty-eight founders, William Cooper and James Smithies. Abraham Greenwood, one of the early members and another giant of cooperation, was also part of the group.

The committee's recommendations were adopted, and a small subscription was raised to pay for further efforts. A subcommittee was appointed to propose legislation to E. V. Neale, the great friend and legislative champion of the cooperative movement. The fight had begun!

Percy Redfern, author of *The Story of the Co-operative Wholesale Society,* wrote about the group:

With all their differing individualities, there was a remarkable bond of common character between all these founders of the Co-operative Wholesale Society. Independence with them was a passion. If they wanted money it was not for lucre's sake, but that they might enjoy freedom . . . This mating in them of qualities derived from the soil and Christian ethics was to be represented by the matter of fact yet idealistic structure they now meant to build.

By late June of 1861, R. A. Slaney, M.P., had brought the bill desired by cooperators before the House of Commons. Richard Cobden, M.P. for Rochdale, was a major backer and John Bright, then M.P. for Manchester, was on hand to assist. However, delays due to Slaney's ill health prevented its passage that year. The next year, the Rochdale Co-op sent James Smithies and Abraham Greenwood to London to lobby for passage. Slaney was too ill, and Bright had to gain the services of another M.P., J. Southeron Estcourt, to carry the bill.

Support of both the Conservatives and Liberals was assured, and after slight amendment, the bill passed both houses and received royal assent. The law still had its imperfections. Although co-op societies now had freedom to invest, they were limited to investing no more than two hundred pounds in another society.

On Christmas Day, 1862, the cooperators once again gave up their holiday to meet in the King Street store of the Oldham Co-op. This time it was to be a joyful occasion, for victory was theirs! It was reported that "one thousand six hundred postal communications," including letters, petition forms, fund requests, and circulars, had been sent to Parliament by co-op activists during the two-year effort.

By Easter of 1863, the cooperators were ready to do business. They met in Manchester, numbering two hundred delegates from all over England. A motion was passed to establish the North of England Co-operative Agency and Depot Society Limited. "A more delightful meeting of Co-operators I never attended," said a correspondent in the pages of the May 1863 Co-operator. By the end of that year, forty-eight societies had joined, almost a quarter of those in existence in England at the time. In 1864 the Co-operative Wholesale Society would begin business. Although there were to be many ups and downs in the early years, the Cooperative Wholesale Society sustained almost continuous growth for decades.

The coming of age of the Co-operative Wholesale Society

is probably best reflected in its role as one of the key supporters of the Manchester Ship Canal. Since 1882, the Co-operative Wholesale Society had subscribed annual organizational expenses for the promotion of the canal. In fact, to show its confidence in the Canal company, the Co-operative Wholesale Society bought ordinary rather than preference shares, and lent 20,000 pounds to the project. In his *History of the Manchester Ship Canal*, Sir Bosdin Leech stated, "This [co-op support] was in marked contrast to the tardy support given by many leading merchants and capitalists of the district, who either held aloof entirely, or contributed the smallest sum that money would allow."

In 1885, John Mitchell, Chairman of the Co-operative Wholesale Society, gave testimony in favor of the canal at hearings at the House of Lords in Westminster. Mitchell believed it was a critical advancement for both the commerce and people of northern England. Almost thirty years earlier, Mr. T. Livesy spoke on behalf of Rochdale to a similar parliamentary select committee that was looking at the costs of local shipping charges to inland towns. He stated that Rochdale was paying Liverpool 4,100 pounds annually for import and export duties.

Queen Victoria opened the canal on January 1, 1894. Ten thousand people from Rochdale went to Manchester to participate in the celebration. The Co-operative Wholesale Society's own steamship, *S. S. Pioneer*, was given the right to lead the first convoy though the canal. The honor of wheeling off the first case of sugar was given to John Mitchell, the Chairman of the Co-operative Wholesale Society, who had never wavered in his support for the canal. From then on, ocean-going ships from every corner of the world were able to sail into the heart of industrial Manchester. The savings to the Co-operative Wholesale Society in both shipping costs and transportation time were substantial. No longer did everything have to be off-loaded in Liverpool and then sent by railroad to the Co-operative Wholesale Society warehouses in Manchester.

In 1884, a joint delegation from the Co-operative Wholesale Society and the Scottish Co-operative Wholesale Society visited the United States and Canada. On this trip, Mitchell, the delegation leader, outlined his dream to unite the purchasing power of the British, Canadian, and U.S. consumer cooperative movements though the Co-operative Wholesale Society depots in each country. His proudest moment occurred when he presented the balance sheet of the Co-operative Wholesale Society to U.S. President Grover Cleveland.

The Immense Contribution of John Mitchell to Consumer Cooperatives

The role of John Mitchell is intertwined forever with the early growth and success of the Co-operative Wholesale Society and its rise to prominence as Britain's largest wholesaler and one of the country's largest employers. His practical impact on the movement towers over that of any other British cooperator.

Mitchell was born in Rochdale in 1828. His grandfather had been a member of the earlier co-op store at 15 Toad Lane and of the Owenite Queenwood Community. Mitchell joined the Rochdale Pioneers in 1853, when he was twenty-four. He served on its management committee in 1856 and later on its library committee. He attended the adult classes given by the Pioneers, a benefit he never forgot. He was secretary to the Pioneers' arts and sciences classes for over fifteen years. When the Borough of Rochdale merged the co-op classes into its Municipal Technical School, Mitchell became the first secretary and served in that role until his death.

For the first forty years of his life, Mitchell belonged mostly to Rochdale. In 1869, he was elected to the board of the Co-operative Wholesale Society, and he was chairman from 1874 until his death in 1895. He was nicknamed "Baron Wholesale" because of the immense power he held as chairman of the Co-operative Wholesale Society. Beatrice Webb and others would say that it was his views that defined the theory of consumer cooperation. Mitchell debated frequently with other co-op leaders at the Co-operative Congresses and other large meetings. He was favorable to neither workers' cooperatives nor workers' domination of consumer cooperatives. On this topic, he engaged in many debates with the Christian Socialists. For one of the best accounts of this critical period of cooperative practice and philosophy, consult

Philip Backstrom's masterpiece, *Christian Socialism and Co-operation in Victorian England.*

When he died, Mitchell had achieved greatness and respect. The coffin at Milton Church in Rochdale where he taught Sunday school was covered in flowers from cooperators and school children. Redfern recounts, "An enormous concourse went to the grave or lined the streets to watch the long procession. Not since the death of John Bright had Rochdale born such witness." He had been born, lived there his whole life, and then had died there. From a humble—and likely illegitimate—birth, and a childhood spent in a beerhouse, he had risen to become one of England's most powerful merchant voices. As an idealistic young man with practical qualities, he had achieved more of his dreams for working people than almost any other progressive leader of his time.

On his grave in the Rochdale Cemetery, the Co-operative Wholesale Society erected a granite monument on which is engraved the following passage from one of Mitchell's addresses:

> The three great forces for the improvement of mankind are religion, temperance, and Co-operation; and as a commercial force, supported and sustained by the other two, Co-operation is the grandest, noblest, and most likely to be successful in the redemption of the industrial classes.

"The romance of the wholesale side of the movement," says Catherine Webb in *Industrial Co-operation*, "is not in its inception, but in its marvelous growth and expansion, and in the possibilities that yet lie before it. But for being illuminated with the cooperative spirit and enthusiasm of the founders, its origins might also be counted a commonplace evolution of sound commercial practice."

The Growth of Cooperative Enterprise Through Unity

The Co-operative Wholesale Society continued at a fast pace during the latter part of the nineteenth century. The Co-operative Wholesale Society played other major roles as it expanded the organization to serve the needs of the millions of consumers who patronized its member societies. The following activities depict the vigorous growth of the Co-operative Wholesale Society—

♦ **Production**
   In 1873, the Co-operative Wholesale Society began production of items to be sold in co-op stores with the introduction of Co-operative Wholesale Society biscuits and shoes. Eventually the Co-operative Wholesale Society entered into the manufacture of almost every domestic product the cooperatives sold. Among these were bread, flour, jams, clothing, furniture, and soap. The Co-operative Wholesale Society makes 60 percent of its own brand goods in its own factories. Today the Co-operative Wholesale Society has twenty factories operating throughout most of England.

♦ **Farming**
   The Co-operative Wholesale Society continued the co-op's long-term interest in food purity and quality by purchasing estates not only in Britain, but throughout the world. As a result, the Co-operative Wholesale Society is now Britain's largest commercial farmer, with over 45,000 acres of cultivated land. The Co-op's "Farm World" near Leicester is Britain's biggest working Farm Park visited by thousands of people yearly.

♦ **Dairy**
   In its early stages, the Co-operative Wholesale Society developed contracts with Danish and Irish creameries to supply butter to the British cooperatives. While the Co-operative Wholesale Society encouraged development of an Irish farmers' cooperative movement, the relationship between them became unworkable. To ensure its dairy supply, the Co-operative Wholesale Society entered the creamery business in 1896. In the twentieth century, the cooperatives were to become Britain's major milk distributor, providing one-third of the households with their daily milk.

♦ Banking

In the 1870s, the Co-operative Wholesale Society had to engage in major efforts to manage its cash flows. Limited by laws on investments by and in other cooperatives, the Co-operative Wholesale Society set up a Credit Agency to administer its millions of pounds in cash. By 1872, the Co-operative Wholesale Society had set up a Loan and Deposit Department, which existed until 1876, when legal restrictions were removed and the Co-operative Wholesale Society Bank was founded. Over time, the bank became the main deposit institution of the cooperative societies, trade unions, working men's clubs, and other popular institutions. Thousands of cooperators and trade unionists became depositors, and from 1909 to 1929 the bank's deposits rose from three million pounds to forty million pounds.

Today the bank, now called The Co-operative Bank, is the most innovative bank in Britain. Its commitment to putting the consumer first, in both philosophy and practice, has won it numerous awards. Its recent commitment to an ethical policy has proved very popular. The Co-op Bank has the largest in-store banking network in Europe. It scores highest of Britain's banks for customer satisfaction and recommendation.

♦ Insurance

The idea that co-op members and societies might develop their own insurance service had been raised for decades before the Co-operative Wholesale Society was founded. The idea began to take shape on Good Friday, April 19,1867, at a meeting in a co-op store in Manchester. Delegates representing 65 cooperative societies in the Manchester region met to review the insurance needs of 151 societies that had participated in a survey. The delegates decided to proceed with the establishment of an insurance company, which was registered on August 29, 1867. The board of directors was elected at the first official meeting, which was held on November 16, 1867.

The first office was registered at the Pioneers' Buildings on Toad Lane in Rochdale until 1871, when it was moved to the Co-operative Wholesale Society in Manchester. Charles Howarth and two other directors from Rochdale were three of the original seven directors. The company went to work immediately, insuring the co-op stores against fire and property damage. Other lines of business insurance were soon added, because the co-ops had diverse insurance needs which they preferred to meet through their own company. In response to member demands for coverage, individual life insurance was added in the 1880s.

The Co-operative Insurance Society has gone on to become one of the most important insurance companies in Britain. Today Co-operative Insurance Society holds 9 billion pounds in assets on behalf of its over four million families, one of the largest market shares in the U.K. Co-operative Insurance Society's staff of 12,500 are based at 224 locations throughout the UK. Not only has the Co-operative Insurance Society flourished in Britain, but it also has played an important role in assisting the development of other cooperative insurance societies throughout the world, particularly in former British colonies.

The Co-operative Union

The Co-operative Union was formed in 1869 to link together the interests of the many societies and to assist in the development of new co-ops. The Co-operative Union has evolved as a national coordinating, advisory, and information body of the cooperative movement. The union also participates in many international cooperative conferences, and monitors political and legislative activity. All co-ops in Britain are eligible to join, and almost every sector is a member. The Co-operative Union holds an annual Co-operative Congress, which is the Co-op Movement's Parliament. A thousand delegates are expected to attend the Co-operative Congress in Rochdale during the anniversary year of 1994.

The Co-operative Union is responsible for the Co-operative College at Stanford Hall near Loughborough. The Co-operative College is an educational charity dedicated to the memory of the Rochdale Pioneers. The College conducts a varied range of both short and long courses, some that focus on education and others that focus on management. The College offers advanced studies in management policy and postgraduate diploma courses in international development.

The Co-operative Party

Owing to various forms of legislative discrimination and attacks against their legislative and tax status, cooperators in Britain often needed parliamentary help. Rather than beg to be heard politically, they formed the Co-operative Party in 1919 to give cooperators a voice in Parliament. Today the Co-operative Party is working all the way from the local council to the European Parliament. There are now fourteen Co-operative-Labour members in the House of Commons, five Co-operative-Labour peers, four Co-operative-Labour Euro M.P.s, and many hundreds of Co-operative-Labour members of municipal councils. John Beasley, Mayor of Rochdale for 1994-1995 is sponsored by the Co-operative Party.

The International Co-operative Alliance

The International Co-operative Alliance was founded in 1895 in London. Much of the early leadership which created the International Co-operative Alliance came from the Christian Socialist group working with the British cooperative movement. E. V. Neale in particular gave tremendous effort to get the International Co-operative Alliance going.

By the end of the 150th anniversary year, there will be over 100 countries represented at the International Co-operative Alliance through over 200 organizations. In 1844 there were 28 members who started the co-op in Rochdale; by 1944 there were 72 million members of the International Co-operative Alliance; and by the end of 1994, there will be 720 million members in the International Co-operative Alliance member organizations. A tenfold increase in fifty years is amazing growth for an idea 150 years old.

The International Co-operative Alliance represents the

interests of the world's cooperatives from their headquarters in Geneva, Switzerland, and through a number of regional offices. The International Co-operative Alliance's membership comes from every sector of the business world and every part of the globe.

New Lanark in Scotland, the model village created by Robert Owen in the early 1800's is visited by over 100,000 people a year. Owen, a practical Utopian, was the founder of the first wave of cooperatives in Britain in the 1820's and 1830's. He is known for initiating laws on childhood education, health and labor conditions, model factories and communities. New Lanark, now an historical site, preserves one of the most successful community experiments of the industrial age.

The Rochdale Society of Equitable Pioneers opened for business on December 21, 1844. The first modern cooperative began as a humble shop with five items for sale: flour, sugar, oatmeal, butter, and candles. When the co-op opened on the ground floor of 31 Toad Lane in Rochdale, England, it set in motion a model of mutual self-help. In 1994 there were 722 million members of cooperatives worldwide. This drawing by C. W. Chapman was presented to the Cooperative Union on the 125th anniversary of the Pioneers.

On the ground floor of the Pioneers' Museum are a number of exhibits. A popular mural photograph is that of 13 of the remaining Pioneers taken in the 1860's. In front of the mural photograph on the right is Charles Howarth's table. On this table he wrote the Rochdale Principles and developed the ideas leading to the birth of the modern cooperative movement.

The upper two floors of the Pioneers' Museum are now one. In earlier years the upstairs had been the reading room, library, and education center for the co-op. This room is the birthplace of the University Extension and Adult School Movements which revolutionized and popularized education. The delegation from the National Cooperative Business Association of the United States are seen here being greeted by John Beasley, the Mayor of Rochdale during a commemorative dinner held at the time of the 1994 opening ceremonies of the 150th anniversary.

The Co-operative Women's Guild is the most successful women's organization ever to exist in Britain. For over 100 years the Guild has been at the forefront of changing living conditions for women, children, and working people. The work of the Guild helped bring about the vote for women and assured them of their property rights. At its height in 1938 the Guild counted over 83,000 active members. Their legacy is to have educated and trained many of the women in Britain who went on to become town councilors, elected officials, and full and contributing citizens of their communities, their country, and many international organizations.

By the late 1850's, there were hundreds of co-ops all across Britain. Whenever the co-op leaders met they discussed unifying their economic activities. From a meeting at Jumbo Farm, near Rochdale, in 1860, emerged the idea of the Co-operative Wholesale Society. Later the visionary co-op leaders created the Co-operative Bank, the Co-operative Insurance Society, the Co-operative Building Society and the Co-operative Union and were leaders in establishing the International Co-operative Alliance.

One of the original objectives of the Rochdale Pioneers was to establish a cooperative community for their members. They built their first houses in the early 1860's and in 1867-88 constructed a cooperative estate of 84 houses in Rochdale with two of the streets being named Equitable and Pioneers. By the turn of the century, the different cooperative societies in Britain had built nearly 25,000 homes for their members. During this century, the housing programs became too large for the local co-ops and were replaced mainly by government and building society programs.

Ebenezer Howard, the father of the Garden City Movement was struck by the Pioneers' cooperative model and advocated housing, consumer, worker and agricultural cooperatives for a central role in the first Garden City in Letchworth, England. For many years Howard lived in Homesgarth (pictured above), a housing cooperative in Letchworth. One of the legacies of the Pioneers was to take the idea of the model village out of the pockets of the philanthropists and place it in the hands of the people. The cooperators gave impetus to the cooperative housing movement, council housing, and the democratic community.

Sweden and the other Scandinavian nations all have strong cooperative sectors. Pictured here is a Domus department store in Stockholm, one of the nearly 1500 co-op stores in Sweden. There are over 2 million members of Swedish consumer cooperatives and two out of three households are connected with the cooperative movement. KF, the Cooperative Union and Wholesale Society, is the fourth largest company in Sweden and accounts for about 20% of the sales of everyday items.

The Mondragon system of cooperatives in the Basque Region of Spain are renowned worldwide. Through its development bank, an educational institute, an enterprise division, and over 100 self-governed, worker-owned enterprises, Mondragon is a unique success. A Basque priest, Father Jose Maria Arizmendiarrieta, developed the first cooperative in 1956 from reading about the ideas of Robert Owen and the Rochdale Pioneers. With over 3 billion dollars in sales and over 25,000 worker-owners, it is the largest corporation in the Basque Region and the fifteenth largest in Spain.

With over 1.3 million active members and nearly 40 stores nationally, Recreational Equipment Inc., is the largest consumer cooperative in the United States. REI was founded in 1938 to pool the purchasing power of a group of mountaineers in Seattle, Washington, who wanted to import quality climbing gear from Europe. The co-op has grown into one of the leading retailers of recreational goods in the USA. In the photo, a group of REI members and staff take a training course in the Rocky Mountains.

In the United States, the National Cooperative Business Association established a Co-op Year Committee to coordinate the celebrations of the 150th anniversary. The highlight was a Cooperative Economic Summit in Washington, D.C. attended by nearly 200 co-op leaders. As part of the Co-op Year celebrations an NCBA delegation attended the opening ceremonies in Rochdale. The U.S. delegation is seen presenting a number of gifts from the U.S. cooperative movement to the Rochdale Pioneers Museum.

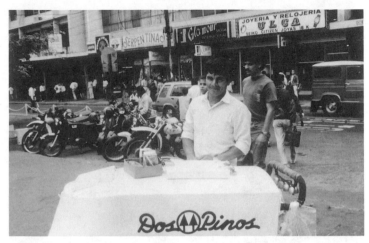

Throughout Latin America there are thousands of cooperatives both large and small serving nearly 14 million members. Here on the streets of San Jose, the capital of Costa Rica, a vendor makes a living selling the products of Dos Pinos. Dos Pinos is a farmer-owned dairy cooperative which markets 60% of the milk production of Costa Rica. The Dos Pinos symbol originated in the United States as Twin Pines and is found throughout the Americas as the symbol of a cooperative.

Oscar Arias, Nobel Peace Prize Winner and former President of Costa Rica, discusses the role of cooperatives with Ann M. Evans at his home in San Jose. Ann is a former Mayor of Davis, California, the founder of the Davis Food Co-op, and spouse of the author. Arias believes strongly that cooperatives build an equitable and democratic economy and are an important tool for developing countries.

Japan is the home of a vibrant and varied consumer cooperative movement with 14 million members. A popular form of consumer cooperative serving over 5 million member families is the Han group, a network of almost one million buying clubs which regularly pool orders. As a group, their order is sent by phone to a main computer at a regional cooperative which then assembles the orders in the warehouse on delivery day.

The Han groups are serviced by regional cooperatives through local warehouses. Every working day, hundreds of delivery vans leave the warehouses on their way to drop off the orders for the neighborhood groups. The vans make a number of trips each day. The volume of the Han groups are now over 10 billion dollars a year. Kanagawa Co-op is engaged in a joint venture with Isuzu to produce the first mid-sized electric delivery van.

Chapter 11

The Revolution in Time

The Impact of the Stamp, the Newspaper,
and the Train

*In truth, it is doubtful whether any single measure passed by
the British Parliament during this century has had a more
potent effect in accelerating the democratic control of our
national life than the cheap and uniform postage invented by
Rowland Hill . . .*
—Beatrice Potter
British Co-operative Movement

The Stamp

The tremendous growth of the Co-operative Movement in
Britain could not have taken place without two other
major changes. The most important was the introduction of
the penny stamp at the General Post Office on May 1, 1840.
What became known as the Penny Black stamp, featuring an
engraving of Queen Victoria, introduced the first national
program of postal service. The Penny Black was the first
postal stamp in the world, with 68,158,080 copies printed. On
May, 23, 1991, a Penny Black stamp with a May 2, 1840,
cover was sold for 1.8 million pounds, the highest price ever
paid for a postage stamp.

In *The Co-operative Movement in Great Britain,* Beatrice
Potter wrote, "Further—and this is a fact of historical signifi-
cance—the penny postage introduced in 1840 secured to
these latter day Co-operators a means of frequent communi-

cation, and rendered feasible, for the first time, the present consolidation of the Co-operative, trade union and political of working men." Success was clear. In 1854, the post office handled 684,047 letters.

The Railway

The development of the railway system was the second major contributor to the growth of the Co-operative Movement. Initially, intense speculation led to abusive fares. Fortunately, the House of Commons passed the Cheap Trains Act of 1844, which required that all railways had to run at least one train per day—each way—with a fare costing no more than a penny a mile. For the first time, people could travel to most parts of Britain easily and cheaply. In a short period the railways revolutionized the meaning of time. Prior to the development of the train, distances of twenty to thirty miles were covered on foot. The first train from Rochdale to Manchester traveled the rails in 1841. By 1856, there were thirteen daily trains to Manchester, ten to Leeds, and eight to Liverpool.

The Liverpool to Manchester Railway opened in 1830 and was the first line to use steam engines exclusively. At that time, 375 miles of track had been constructed in Britain. By 1838 there were 89 railway companies operating approximately 500 miles of track and by 1840 there were nearly 2400 miles constructed. The railway boom was now off and running with railway shares setting the pace for the stock market. By 1848, over 8000 miles of track was in place covering every major area of the country. Over a quarter of a million men were then feverishly building the railroads of Britain.

The railway was a boon to the cooperative organizers because it allowed them to meet regularly with both new and existing cooperatives. It also made conferences easy to arrange, and hundreds—even thousands—of cooperators could gather together to share ideas and develop plans. For example, on September 19, 1862, the Pioneers ran an excursion train to London carrying 308 members who had bought round trip tickets at six shillings. Compare that with the fact that the first stagecoach service from Rochdale to Manchester began in 1767, ninety-five years earlier.

Newly emerging railways and the postal service ensured that the mail, magazines, and newspapers were delivered timely and efficiently to all corners of Britain. The railways were the bustling booster of Britain, signifying the progress and optimism of the times. Trains, more than any other invention, changed the everyday life of working people. The railway bridges, tracks, and tunnels spread to every corner of the country and sped the delivery of goods from the producer to the consumer. The railway system helped to turn the Co-operative Wholesale Society into the most powerful consumer distribution system in Britain. Interestingly, the Co-operative Insurance company invested its early surplus funds in the stock of the burgeoning railway companies.

The Newspaper

The British government placed a prohibitive tax on newspapers, which made their circulation among the general population too expensive. One major reason for the popularity of the Pioneers' reading rooms was that the Pioneers could buy one newspaper for many people to read. Holyoake owed an immense unpayable debt of 600,000 pounds to the government when he died. His crime—having published unstamped newspapers for decades.

Upon his death in 1906, Holyoake was buried in Highgate Cemetery in a grave just opposite Karl Marx. Both their statues exhibit a firm gaze and determination. Both Holyoake and Marx believed wholeheartedly in their own actions and philosophies. Yet Holyoake's statue has his back to Marx. In life, they never saw eye to eye, and in death it had been guaranteed.

Chapter 12

The Basket That Changed Britain

The Successes of the Cooperative Women's Guild

The spirit of co-operation which binds the Guild into one united whole in purpose and action, and gives to the shopping baskets of its members a great power to lift the ordinary commerce of daily existence into a movement for social betterment, is also the spirit which can regenerate the world.
—Catherine Webb
The Woman with the Basket

The women of Rochdale have always been at the forefront of reform. In 1808, when the first political reform meeting in Britain took place at Cronkeyshaw Common near Rochdale, the local newspaper gave this description:

> The procession began to move about 2 o'clock and was headed by at least 5,000 female reformers and followed by 30,000 men bearing but too sad an evidence of the distress of the times . . . The cap of liberty was carried in front with other banners . . . and on a fourth (banner) "Success to Female Societies."

During the 1830s and 1840s, the Chartists and the Anti-Corn Law League were uneasy and infrequent allies. The

Chartists focused on extending the vote to the working class and gaining representation in Parliament. Man could no longer live on bread alone, although the middle-class Anti-Corn League worked hard to reduce the price of flour. In 1839 there was a public meeting in Rochdale to discuss the repeal of the Corn Laws. Although John Bright had called the meeting, the Chartist supporters outnumbered the members of the Anti-Corn Law League and voted in their own chair. The Chartist women had an active role in the takeover of the meeting. As in 1808, the Chartist women usually led the demonstrations and processions. That year (1839) they founded the Female Radical Association to ensure that women would have their own protected forum for debating issues.

When strikes were spreading throughout Lancashire in August of 1842, John Bright wrote, "About 2,000 women paraded the town this morning singing hymns. The men are gone to other towns and villages to turn all the hands out. Has the revolution commenced? It looks very probable. The authorities are powerless."

Holyoake credits Ann Tweedale with playing an important role in helping to organize the co-op. When the co-op organizers needed a regular meeting space, she got them a room at the Labour and Health pub, where her brother, Samuel Tweedale, one of the original Pioneers, was the landlord. She was on the list of an earlier cooperative society which preceded the Pioneers. Did she not have money? Was she living with her family and was the family the member? Were the Pioneers concerned about allowing women members? Why was she not an early member?

Ann Tweedale later married Benjamin Standring (probably a brother or relative of James Standring, one of the Pioneers) and encouraged him to become a member of the co-op. However, married women were restricted by law from owning assets in their own name; Tweedale at the time could not become a member nor own stock in her own right. Keep in mind that there was no cooperative law, nor corporate law as we know it today. Co-op historians such as Percy Redfern do recount that the first person to shop at the store was a woman. History has its own way of bestowing honor.

December of 1844 also saw the founding of the Rochdale Protestant Female Friendly Sick and Burial Society, which met at the White Lion Inn on Yorkshire Street. In those days, friendly societies were created informally as a simple sort of group insurance and mutual assistance. This group was possibly the first and only female mutual enterprise in Rochdale at the time.

In those days, the males of the upper class governed society through their ownership of land and the major resources and control of the key institutions. Society's rules on ownership precluded women from owning shares in their own right and keeping their own bank accounts. W. Henry Brown inspected the records of the privately owned Rochdale Savings Bank, which failed in 1849. Of the bank's members, 271 were men and only 14 were women (probably they were widows).

Dr. Ann Hoyt at the University of Wisconsin has a longtime interest in the role of women in cooperatives. She comments on this subject:

The invisibility of women has had a devastating effect in all of the countries whose systems are based upon English Common Law. The principle has been used consistently in the United States, for example, to deny equal distribution of assets in case of divorce. To me, one of the most wonderful moments in the Rochdale Pioneer's history is that the co-op intentionally broke the law and allowed women to accumulate capital in their own right. The co-op protected the women's right to keep their capital even when their husbands demanded it. This often provided the cushion these women needed to escape dire poverty.

For a description of the effects, read *Life As We Have Known It,* edited by M. L. Davies, originally published by the Women's Co-operative Guild.

At the turn of the century, women and men were joining co-ops in Britain in equal number. By June of 1944, of the 271 persons joining the Pioneers, 159 were women and 112 were men.

In February of 1861, Mr. Ambrose Tomlinson, an activist,

provided material for a short history of the co-op to a local newspaper, *The Rochdale Spectator*. Tomlinson gave *The Spectator* the book of the association that preceded the co-op that was being formed. Many members of that association were among the twenty-eight Pioneers. The list of members of this earlier co-op includes two women, Ann Tweedale and Mary Bromley.

According to Roy Garrett, Curator of the Rochdale Museum, the first woman accepted as a member of the Pioneers Society (in 1846) was Eliza Brierley. The records show that Ms. Brierley showed up and paid her three-pound share in full. Garratt credits G. J. Holyoake as a great cooperator but a factually incorrect writer who gave too much credit to Ann Tweedale, and he points out that her name never appeared in the Rochdale record book of members. As we can see, there are many reasons from the era which would ensure that her name is missing from the list.

Ann Tweedale is to the Co-operative Movement a little like the unknown soldier. She represents so many who fought without recognition. We keep her name alive because she is the only woman that historians give any credit to for actively getting the co-op started. On the other hand, as with the unknown soldier, we know little to nothing about her. We therefore keep her name alive as an eternal representative of the role of women in starting and supporting the Co-operative Movement. We know that women played an important role, but we also know that male society of the era scorned activist women and the historians of the day ignored their contributions. The name of Ann Tweedale celebrates the contribution of the women who helped start the co-op in Rochdale and all the women who invisibly are a part of the starting of so many co-ops.

Women took many roles in the creation of the co-op. Who got the dinner ready at night, who put the kids to bed, who waited up to see how the meeting went, who understood better than anyone what a co-op could do, who went without to buy the co-op share, who loyally shopped at the co-op even though there was little on the shelves? Who shopped for cash when credit would have fed the children that day? Who sewed the staff aprons and spread the word, who were the missionaries and who carried the heavy basket home? Who had a voice yet no vote? And don't forget most women were also working a long day. Could any one of the Pioneers have put in the time were it not for the backing of his wife?

William Cooper, a founding Pioneer, wrote a short history of the Co-operative Corn Mill Society in which he included a passage which priaised the role of women in co-ops:

The wife, who is mostly as good a supporter of the Mill as her husband, generally putting up with the flour when it was not so good as it ought to be, and often, when she had a nice baking of bread, showing it to all neighbours and comers—that they might be convinced what good flour the Corn Mill Society was making. Certainly some husbands would find fault with the wife when the bread was not good, and say she had spoiled the flour, to which some wives would reply, they could bake as well as other people if they had the same flour, and that they would not use the Corn Mill Society's flour if they were to be grumbled at because they could not make good bread out of bad flour. We have said the husband would be from home while attending meetings, and may be, the wife had put the children to bed, and would be waiting with no one to speak a word to her, until the husband came from the meeting. All would be silent except the constant tick of the clock, the rain battering against the windows, and the wind whistling and howling as if it had risen in revolt against the restraints imposed upon it by nature. To the wife alone, minutes seem as long as hours, she thinks she is neglected, her husband attending meetings or anything else rather than home. At another time little Elizabeth has been sickly some days, and father has been at work all day, and now, when his work is done, has gone to the meeting. The mother cannot get the child to rest— she thinks it is getting worse. When the husband comes home, she tells him how sickly the child is, and that he ought not to have gone to the meeting—indeed if he had any thought for the child he could not go. He tells her he has come home as soon as the meeting was over, but he cannot persuade her that he ought to have gone at all. He believes the child will be better in a few days, and promises to help her to nurse and take care of it till it is so. These, or many similar incidents, will have occurred to most persons engaged in promoting social or other reforms. But it must not be said that the women are opposed to Co-operation; no, they are, and ever have been, as much interested and as zealous of its success as the men. There are many instances where the husband was lukewarm, and the wife could not prevail on him to join the Co-operative Societies, but she was not to be baffled, so she enters the Co-operative Societies herself.

Near Rochdale, just ten miles away on the other side of the Pennines, is the town of Ripponden in Yorkshire. Since 1832, the Ripponden Co-operative Society has laid claim to the title of the oldest continuing cooperative society in the world. It is one of those co-ops that began with the first wave initiated by Owen. I will, however, leave this question to other historians. In the centenary history of the society published in 1932, the author, John H. Priestley, challenged Rochdale's claim to fame:

On the question of admitting females into the movement we also find the Pioneers much behind the Ripponden Society. They had an application from a women to become a member in 1846, and were diffident about admitting her. Not till February, 1847, did they admit another, nearly three years from the commencement.

Ripponden on the other hand admitted three women within three months, and seven within two years, and in 1842, two years before the Pioneers had begun, they had nineteen female members. Ripponden recognized the strength of the "women with the basket" in good time. The writer [of a brochure by the Rochdale Pioneers] is mistaken in saying that the first women admitted by the Pioneers in 1846 and 1847 were the first to venture into the shareholding lists of modern Co-operation. Margaret and Rachel Mathews and Sarah Whiteley, who joined the Ripponden Society in 1833, were the first women on the shareholding list of modern Co-operation.

The women's movement of the 1850s and beyond focused mainly on the lives of middle-class women who complained that the conditions for middle-class women were oppressive and purposeless. These women were educated, but they could not vote and had few rights. They were intellectually developed, but had no real voice. They were as competent as men, but were excluded from roles in business and politics. They knew they could shine, but were relegated to the shadows of society. At the height of their suffocation they looked to free their new consciousness. The time had come to act!

The co-op also was pushed to take a role in educating women. Mary, the youngest daughter of James Smithies, was encouraged by her father to apply to the Pioneers to use the library. She became the first women to use the (then) exclusively male Pioneers' library. Mary was a teacher and eventually became headmistress of Derby Street School in Rochdale. She became the first president of the Rochdale Women Teachers' Association formed in 1917.

The issues related to the Industrial Revolution, class differences, and poverty were central to the times. In the period beginning with the 1840s and 1850s, the social novel and the protest novel entered literature. More importantly, women writers were making a breakthrough. In just over a decade, the following protest novels by women were published: Frances Trollope's *Michael Armstrong the Factory Boy* (1840), Elizabeth Gaskell's *Mary Barton* (1848) and *North and South* (1854), Charlotte Bronte's *Shirley* (1849), Helen Tonna's *Helen Fleetwood* (1849), and Geraldine Jewsbury's *Marian Withers* (1851).

Novels by women writers differed from those authored by men in that they featured women as central characters and highlighted issues of concern to women. These novelists wrote from a feminist perspective and saw society through the eyes of women. Because they came from the middle class, the writers represented the perspectives prevalent in middle-class society. They avoided urging revolution by the working class, although they wrote of the agonies the working class suffered. They pleaded with the manufacturing classes and the new middle class to be considerate of the workers. They hoped that a woman's voice infused with the values of family, community, and caring would be heard and would modify promotion of individuality and isolation by the manufacturing class. The women writers hoped for a peaceful resolution of the differences in society through reducing the excesses of the era.

The women writers of the 1800s continued a tradition begun by their counterparts in the 1700s. Sarah Scott, author of *Millennium Hall* (1762), writes about a woman's Utopia. At Millennium Hall the women are no longer chattel to the male world and without voice. They choose to create a cooperative community committed to a life of equality, participation, and friendship. In conducting research on this hidden part of history, Alessa Johns states, "Their utopias become places where they can overcome financial difficulties, retain their class position, contribute to the common good, and simultaneously maintain their independence." While they are all of independent means, they see the inequality of society. They pursue education as a foundation for income and finance a factory where people in the village have good working conditions and pay.

However, by the 1840s there is no longer an idealized Utopia to give comfort. The impact of industrialized society had brought a new reality to the same concerns and a hard edge to women's writing. In *North and South,* by Elizabeth Gaskell, the mill owner is challenged by the heroine:

> "Mr. Thornton," said Margaret, shaking all over with her passion, "go down this instant, if you are not a coward. Go down and face them like a man. Save these poor strangers whom you have decoyed here. Speak to your workmen as if they were human beings. Speak to them kindly. Don't let the soldiers come in and cut down the poor creatures who are driven mad."

The theme of woman writers appealing for justice and understanding continues to the present.

The difficulties and obstacles for women of that era were numerous. The efforts of the Pioneers were to make a difference. One of the Pioneers' important contributions to women's rights was the role the Pioneers played in the passage of the Married Women's Property Rights Act in 1870. Almost from the beginning, the Pioneers made no distinction as to who could own shares, but prior to 1870 the law held that a married woman's property legally belonged to her husband. The Pioneers ignored the law and protected the rights of their shareholders, be they male or female. If a man demanded the share or dividends of his wife, he was refused and the wife was informed of his attempt to take her money.

The British Home Secretary, Mr. Bruce (later Lord Aberdare), was told about this policy by Professor Stuart of Cambridge University. The Home Secretary sent his private secretary, Albert Rutson, to Rochdale. Rutson talked with the women in the store and inspected the society's records. He was impressed by what he saw and heard, and returned to London to report positively on his visit. It was mainly owing to Rutson's visit that women's property rights became the law of the land.

One of the most important women in Britain at the time got her start studying the growing Co-operative Movement. Beatrice Potter was a young social researcher who took a keen interest in Cooperatives. In 1883 she began researching the institutions of working-class life in Lancashire. In the beginning, she posed as Miss Jones because the Potter family were too well known in South Lancashire. Her father, Richard Potter, was an industrialist and railway magnate. One uncle, Thomas Bayley Potter, a former M.P. for Rochdale, has already been mentioned. Coming from a powerful political family and an upper-middle-class manufacturing background, she would likely be suspect in the parlors of the poor weavers.

Beatrice Potter often gave papers at Co-operative and trade union meetings. She gave her first major address to the Co-operative Congress at Rochdale in 1892. In 1889 she began writing *The Cooperative Movement,* which for many years was the only impartial study of the progress of the consumer cooperatives. Later she married Sidney Webb, another rising star, forming one of the most influential and enduring political partnerships in Britain. Together they played a critical role in founding the Fabian Society and the London School of Economics and in reforming the British Labour Party. They co-authored a book, *The Consumers Cooperative Movement,* published in 1921. The Webbs remained co-op supporters all of their lives. In her later years, Beatrice Webb traveled in the most powerful circles in the nation, as well as the globe. She remained an inspiration to the many women in the Co-operative Movement who pursued education as a means to progress. Those humble, hard-working women never forgot the young woman's speech at Rochdale in 1892 to a hall mostly full of men. The women were made proud and no longer afraid.

In 1883, Mrs. Alice Ackland lit the spark for organizing women members of cooperatives to play a larger role. She was invited by Samuel Bamford, the editor of *The Co-operative News,* to write a column titled "Women's Corner." Ackland wrote:

> What are men always urged to do when there is a meeting held at any place to encourage or to start Co-operative institutions? Come! Help! Vote! Criticize! Act! What are women urged to do? Come and Buy! ... To come and buy is all we can be asked to do; but cannot we go further ourselves? Why should we not have our meetings, our readings, our discussions?

Ideas began to pour into *The Co-operative News.* One woman wrote:

> Women want more changes than they have now; they want taking away from the cares of the home for a time, and I think there ought to be meetings held at the store expressly for women . . . so that we could converse together on Co-operation.

In 1883, as a result of the interest, the Co-operative Women's Guild was born. Within a short time there were hundreds of branches throughout Britain.

D. H. Lawrence captured the impact of the Co-operative Women's Guild on working-class women in a passage from his novel, *Sons and Lovers:*

> When the children were old enough to be left, Mrs. Morel joined the Women's Guild. It was a little club of women attached to the Co-operative Wholesale Society, which met on Monday night in the long room over the grocery shop of the Bestwood Co-op. The women were supposed to discuss the benefits of Co-operation, and other social questions. Sometimes Mrs. Morel read a paper. It seemed queer to the children to see their mother, who was always busy about the house, sitting writing in her rapid fashion, thinking, referring to books and writing again. They felt for her on such occasions the deepest respect.
>
> But they loved the Guild. It was the only thing to which they did not begrudge their mother—and that partly because she enjoyed it, partly because of the treats they derived from it. The Guild was called by some hostile husbands, who found their wives getting too independent, the clat-fart shop—that is the gossip shop. It is true, from the basis of the Guild, the women could look at their homes, or at the conditions of their own lives, and find fault. So the colliers found their women had a new standard of their own rather disconcerting. And also, Mrs. Morel always had a lot of news on Monday nights, so that the children liked William [the eldest son] to be in when their mother came home, because she told them things.

Votes for Women

Between 1832 and 1884, three reform bills had been passed. While they made some changes in voting requirements, the laws still based voting rights on levels of male property ownership. Out of a Rochdale population of 28,000 in 1832, only 687 males had voting rights. In the 1832 elections 632 males voted, and in the 1840 elections only 734 voted. Arguing in Parliament in 1866 for extension of the voting franchise, John Bright, M.P., used the example of the Rochdale Pioneers and their responsible use of the vote. In replying, William Gladstone commented that the town of Rochdale "probably has done more than any other town in making good to practical minds a case for some enfranchisement of the working-classes." It would not be until 1884 that a majority of property owners finally won the right to vote.

In 1915, the Guild published *Maternity: Letters from Working Women*. This was the first ever presentation of the working women's view of maternity. "Do publish these letters . . . they are so amazing," wrote Virginia Woolf to her friend, Margaret Llewelyn Davies. The collection of letters, which had been assembled as part of a campaign by the Guild for maternity benefits, stunned the middle class into action. By applying pressure, the Guild won a thirty shilling maternity benefit. More importantly, in 1913 the Guild established that legally, the benefit was the property of the mother.

It was not until 1918 that universal suffrage in national elections was extended to everyone except women under thirty. Women had to wait another ten years to have the same rights as men. Were it not for the suffragettes, the Co-operative Women's Guild, and the role of women in World War I, it probably would have taken longer. Out of suffering often comes beauty. During the First World War, it was suggested to Hubert Parry that he write suitable simple music to William Blake's poem, "Jerusalem." People were hungry for a song that an audience could join in. The result was the magnficent unison song, "Jerusalem," that is now a second national anthem. It was first performed at a Votes for Women concert in 1916 and has never stopped stirring audiences.

One of the early issues taken up by the Guild was that of women's suffrage. In 1893, the middle-class suffrage societies organized a giant petition, which was signed by a quarter of a million women; one-quarter of the Guild members were signatories. But, as before, the petition failed. Guild members were then urged to take action at the local level. In 1894, forty-five Guild members ran for election as Poor Law Guardians, and twenty-two were successful. From that beginning, Guild members felt encouraged to run for various other locally elected offices.

◆

By 1927, over seven hundred Guild women had been either elected or appointed to public office in Britain. The Guild had taken the "Woman with the Basket" to a very different role in society. Catherine Webb's book by that name documents the victories of the Co-operative Women's Guild. The women who were changing their co-ops were now prepared to change Britain.

By the turn of the century, over half the members of British consumer cooperatives were women. By 1930, sixty-two thousand women were active members of the Guild through the local branches. Because co-op members were generally from the artisan class, their wives had hopes for the future. Theirs was the generation and class who saw that life would change for the better. The key to the world beyond the row house was education and organization. The Guild became Britain's pre-eminent women's organization and compiled an enviable record of success in parliament centered on issues of importance to women, children, and the welfare state. For decades it was the strongest organization working on behalf of the voteless and voiceless women of Britain.

In 1933, the Guild celebrated its Jubilee Year. The highlight was a rally at the Crystal Palace in London at which fifteen thousand women gathered together in unity to sing their hymns, hear speeches, and parade with their banners. The Guild's former General Secretary, Margaret Llewelyn Davies, urged them ". . . not to be content with [their] triumphs but to go forward . . . " At the outbreak of World War II, the Guild membership had risen to 1,819 branches and 87,246 individuals, its highest ever.

There is one woman, Margaret Llewelyn Davies, who will forever be remembered for her devotion and contribution to the success of the Guild. Born in 1861, she became Secretary of the Marylebone, London, branch of the Guild in 1886 and was elected to the Central Committee in 1888. She became General Secretary in 1889 and served in that position until she retired in 1921. Her father was a reformer, Christian Socialist, honorary chaplain to the Queen, and an activist in developing the Working Men's College. When her father was appointed Vicar of Kirkby Lonsdale in West Yorkshire in 1889, the whole family moved there.

Educated at Queen's College, London, and Girton College, Oxford, Ms. Davies studied education and feminist emancipation. When the family moved to Kirkby Lonsdale in the moors of West Yorkshire in 1889 the Guild moved there, too. All of the activities of the Guild were conducted from a small room in the rural vicarage. For over 30 years she and Lilian Harris, her loyal friend and Assistant Secretary of the Guild, served there without pay. Ms. Davies never married, she committed her life to the Guild and to the Co-operative Movement. She was known as a powerful speaker, a great presence, and an untiring organizer.

She helped found the International Women's Guild Committee in 1921 in Basel, Switzerland. Her greatest honor was being elected President of the Co-operative Congress in 1922, the first woman ever to reach this position. She died in 1944, Rochdale's centenary. Her memorial meeting, held on June 15, 1944 at the Co-operative Wholesale Society Assembly Hall in Manchester, was described in *The Cooperative News* as "Not a service of mourning, not even great sorrow. Rather there was a spirit of thanksgiving for a noble life of service and gratitude for the privilege of having known her and shared in the work she inspired."

It was not until 1975, the International Year of the Woman, that Eva M. Dodds, a Co-operative Wholesale Society Director, became the second woman to be elected president of the Co-operative Congress. Nora E. Willis was the third—elected in 1983 in honor of the 100th Anniversary of the Guild—and Gladys Bunn became the fourth woman president, elected at the 1987 Blackpool Congress.

After the war ended, Britain would undergo the greatest changes it would experience in the twentieth century. To the surprise of many in 1945, a majority Labour Government was elected for the first time.

An elated Aneurin Bevan, an M.P. and soon to be cabinet minister in the new Labour Government, stated "We have been the dreamers, we have been the sufferers, and now we are the builders." His wife, Jennie Lee, also an activist Labour M.P., was a lifetime supporter of the Co-operative Movement. The nation was ready to adopt massive changes in social policy, education, welfare, health, and housing.

What the Guild had been urging Parliament and the nation to do for decades was now achieved overnight. In a post-war Britain, society was being radically restructured. With a government committed to the same goals as the Guild, there was now less reason for the Guild. With retailing also undergoing a massive reformation, the co-ops were being forced to merge rapidly to ensure that they remained competitive, leaving fewer co-op organizations around to sponsor the local Guilds. A sympathetic Labour Government and the merging of societies brought about a continued decline in the Guild membership.

But the Guild's decline should not be viewed as failure. The Guild had been the most successful women's group in Britain and the only mass working-class women's organization. The Guild served as the training ground for women entering public service and politics. It had taken on issues which had changed the face of the nation. Almost all of its social and political objectives had been achieved. "The woman with the basket" carried home from the co-op more than groceries. In their baskets they carried home hopes and dreams, leaflets and petitions. The extras the Guild members took home in that "basket" changed Britain forever.

Chapter 13

Cooperative Education

The Road to Economic Freedom and Democracy

Unless the principles of Co-operative economics are well understood by every member, the Cooperative will ultimately collapse, although outside pressure may hold it together for a while. Accordingly the Cooperative movement must begin with a thorough-going educational movement.
— **Toyohiko Kagawa**
Brotherhood Economics

Providing food during the "hungry forties" was important to keeping people alive, but education was the tool for ensuring that people got ahead. The Pioneers recognized the importance of both strategies for serving the needs of their members. At the time, there was no public education or free library system in England, and the cost of books and newspapers was beyond reach of working people. Working people had few opportunities to move into the skilled positions that would increase their earnings. The Pioneers were clear in their focus; education would ensure that their members could walk towards economic freedom and democracy. If the co-op was to advance its goals of serving millions of working people, it needed educated and competent employees. The goals of the Owenites, Chartists, and other idealists of the era were to create communities filled with educated inhabitants. Education would prepare people for industry and citizenry.

107

The Rochdale store is to the beginning of the Co-operative Movement what Faneuil Hall in Boston is to the birth of the United States of America. On the ground floor of both historic buildings was an everyday marketplace for food, and on the second floor the marketplace for revolutionary ideas. Knowledge, education, public meetings, debates, and dissent were the currents and currency of the upper floors. As Faneuil Hall fed the mind and bodies of Bostonians during the Revolutionary era, so did the co-op shop in Rochdale during the Industrial Revolution. Shopping for democracy and daily bread were one and the same during the historic beginnings of both movements.

The self-help organizations of cooperatives, political organizations, nonconformist chapels, and civic-minded groups were key to education in the 1800s. The 1833 Factory Act had required that factory owners provide education to their young workers (two hours of schooling and nine hours work for those under thirteen). However, an inspection of 500 mills in the West Riding of Yorkshire in 1838 revealed that only 12 mills had complied with the regulation. As a result, Factory Schools were made compulsory in 1844 and provided three and a half hours of education to all children working in the factories covered by the 1833 Act. Until then, almost all education of the working class had been voluntary and through self-help organizations.

Education was a high priority for the Pioneers. They saw how education allowed people to learn more, earn more, and organize more effectively. The shop at Toad Lane was quickly put to educational uses, especially on Sunday, when the store was closed for business but open for education. The members would turn up to discuss the issues of the day. Founding pioneer Samuel Tweedale gave the first lecture: "Morals in Their Relation to Everyday Life." Another Pioneer, James Smithies, taught writing and arithmetic on Sundays and encouraged his daughters to attend the classes. Knowledge was power, and brains became more important than brute strength. The passport to prosperity was learning, and the skilled co-op members were an artisan aristocracy in search of progress.

Elizabeth Gaskell knew full well of this undercurrent in

society whereby workers relentlessly pursued knowledge. She wrote in her 1848 novel *Mary Barton*:

There is a class of men in Manchester, unknown even to many of the inhabitants, and whose existence will probably be doubted by many, who yet may claim kindred with all the noble names that science recognizes. I said in "Manchester" but they are scattered all over the manufacturing districts of Lancashire. In the neighborhood of Oldham there are weavers, common hand loom weavers, who throw the shuttle with unceasing sound, though Newton's *Principia* lie open on the loom, to be snatched at in work hours, but reveled over in meal times, or at night. Mathematical problems are received with interest, and studied with absorbing attention by many a broad-spoken, common looking factory hand.

In order to have a space for discussions and classes, the co-op took over the upper part of the building, vacated by the Bethel Chapel, when it became available in June of 1849. The rental for the entire building was fixed at twenty-three pounds per year. James Daly, the joiner, was allocated 200 pounds to re-fixture the front of the store. The top floor became a tailoring department and a clog and cobbler's shop.

The Pioneers' Library

The co-op turned the second story into a reading room and began developing a library. Books were then too expensive for working people to purchase, and there were no free libraries. On August 20, 1849, it was resolved by the Board

that Messrs. James Nuttall, Henry Green, Abraham Greenwood, George Adcroft, James Hill and Robert Taylor be a committee to open a stall for the sale of books, periodicals, newspapers, etc.; the profits to be applied to the furnishing of the members room with newspapers and books.

Thus began the cooperative's education department. In 1850, the People's Institute, a middle-class literary society, failed, and their library of 1,100 books was immediately purchased by the Pioneers.

The progress of the co-op's educational activities was aided immensely by the acquisition of both the books and the librarian of the People's Institute, Abraham Greenwood. A member of the co-op since 1846, Greenwood went on to become one of the great co-op leaders of England. It was Greenwood who drew up the scheme for the Co-operative Wholesale Society and became its first president.

By 1862, the Pioneers' library collection had grown to five thousand volumes, and use was now free. In December of 1869, John Bright donated 750 books from his library to the Pioneers Society, and in 1870, a library of nine thousand volumes was opened in the new Central Store. After one year at the new location, the library had grown to seventeen thousand volumes. By then, eleven reading rooms had been opened at other co-op stores located throughout Rochdale.

As a result, the co-op became the foremost educational institute in Rochdale. Years later, Karl Marx commented, that in all of Britain, the library and newsroom of the Rochdale Pioneers was second only to that of the British Museum. George Dawson, a popular orator of the period, spoke of his visit to Toad Lane:

> I have seen many libraries—in Rome, Vienna, Paris and Oxford, but the library of libraries was that of the Rochdale Equitable Pioneers. There were libraries with more books and scarcer and more splendid volumes, but the origin of this library was unparalleled in the history of the world.

The Newsroom

The Rochdale Almanac of 1854 described the newsroom thus:

> a bounteously filled room in those days, abounding in dailies, weeklies and quarterlies, was open from nine in the morning to nine at night, at a charge of two pennies per month. This gave an average of 2520 hours reading for two pence.

Working people could not afford both the cost and the tax on regular newspapers. When the co-op moved to the Central Stores in 1867, the Central newsroom was supplied with twenty-seven daily papers, fifty-five weekly papers, and many monthly and quarterly magazines.

In a paper about the origins of the Education Department of the Rochdale Equitable Pioneers' Cooperative Society given in 1877, Abraham Greenwood had this to say:

> The early Pioneers were in the habit of assembling themselves together after the day's toil was done in the back room of the old store, for the purpose of hearing the news of the week . . . News of the day was circulated by word of mouth to a very great extent amongst the working-classes forty years ago, and often gained rather than lost something of the truth in being thus diffused . . . There were certainly some Utopian dreamers amongst the early Pioneers; all of whom were more or less sentimentalists; but while all sentimentalists, they were not necessarily void of common sense to curb that sentiment within the bounds of reason and what was practical . . . Aim high enough in your purpose, and in the attempt at its accomplishment your effort will result in having done some good, if not all the good you proposed to do.

Budgeting for Education

In the beginning, the quarterly meetings of the Pioneers made illegal grants towards education. The Registrar of Friendly Societies had disallowed the Pioneers from allocating 10 percent of the profits to education. John Kershaw, one of the Pioneers, wrote, "These were the days when the law prohibited workmen from educating themselves and the government refused them the franchise on account of their want of knowledge." Upon adoption of the new Industrial and Provident Act of 1853, the co-op set aside 10 percent of its profits to go towards education. The government's Registrar of Friendly Societies disallowed such generosity, and finally agreed to 2.5 percent. An education committee was formed, which was to change the face of education worldwide, and each subsequent co-op shop was designed to include a library and reading room.

The Birth of University Extension

A school for young people operated from 1850 to 1855. Advanced subjects were provided for the mature and inquisitive working-class audience, and the co-op was committed to bringing in distinguished lecturers from all across England. The response was voracious, and people walked miles to attend lectures or classes. People were starving for knowledge, and no one lecture could satiate the appetite of the co-op members—they always wanted more.

Professor Sadler's *Manual on University Extension* stated:

> It was at Rochdale that a Cambridge astronomy professor, Professor Stuart invented "The Class," the period of conversational teaching, enlivened by brief periods of "heckling" which has ever since been an important feature of the University Extension system.

Its origins were simple. Stuart's lectures were illustrated by diagrams which were left on the walls of the co-op until the next meeting. Members attending a general meeting of the society were so attracted to the materials and the concepts that they stayed to discuss them, and they wrote to Professor Stuart asking him to come to the lecture room before the next class so that they might ask him some questions. "He did so, and thus began the first University Extension Class," Sadler adds. Other ties were created between the universities and the cooperatives. This episode provides another example of the leadership of the Rochdale Pioneers. When Beatrice Webb visited the Guild branch at the cooperative in Hebden Bridge in 1881 she recalled, "Young Oxford men are down here; and they and the co-operators form a mutual admiration society between intellectual young Oxford and Cooperative working-class."

In 1873 the Pioneers affiliated with the Science and Art Department of South Kensington, London. This academic relationship allowed the co-op to offer classes in most of the sciences, and it began to rent scientific equipment to its members.

In 1894 the Pioneers decided to discontinue all of its technical classes. In the twenty years since the Pioneers had begun this work, technical education had changed dramatically. The role of educator had been assumed by the state and the local authorities—there was no longer a need for the Pioneers to do what society was now doing. The task of the Pioneers was complete, education was universally available, and the Adult School was in place throughout Britain.

Cooperative Education

During the early decades of the cooperatives, education about cooperatives played a secondary role to education for industry. As the co-op role was filled by the state, cooperators began to focus on Cooperative education.

At earlier cooperative congresses in the 1870s, the idea of a cooperative college had been the dream of a small band of dedicated cooperative educators. The Co-operative Congress of 1898 vastly reorganized the structure and delivery of cooperative education. At the Congress, Albert Mansbridge, an employee of the Co-operative Wholesale Society, made an impassioned plea for the co-op to meet the needs of working-class students. In 1903, he wrote a number of articles on how co-ops, trade unions, and university extension should work together in a more focused program. To support his ideas, he founded the Workers' Educational Association. By the next year, the Oxford Extension Summer Meeting convened a special meeting to discuss Mansbridge's ideas.

In later years, cooperators began to discuss the wider application of cocperative education. In 1909, the Co-operative Union sponsored its first weekend school at the innovative garden city of Letchworth. It seemed fitting that a new town built on cooperative principles and focused on the future should host the school. The first of the annual Easter Education weekends took place the next year, and in 1913 the first summer school convened in Castelton. The growth of the co-op's educational activities brought the vision of a cooperative college ever closer. The college was to educate the board and committee members and the management and staff of cooperatives, to strengthen the organizational and operational

113

capacity of the cooperative movement.

At the 1919 Co-operative Congress, the central board was asked to formulate plans and set a fund-raising goal of fifty thousand pounds. Because the money was slow to come in, it was decided to get the concept started at Holyoake House, the home of the Co-operative Union in Manchester. A hostel was acquired for the students at Kersal in Manchester. For the years 1938 to 1939, there were 1,350 classes and 23,529 students registered with the Co-operative Union Education Department.

The Co-operative College claims to have been the only adult working-class college to remain open during the entire war. During 1944, the centenary year of Rochdale, the education executive initiated an appeal to fund a new Co-operative College with room for one hundred students. A sum of 250,000 pounds was sought and over half was donated in the first months of the appeal. By March of 1945 enough had been raised to purchase Stanford Hall in Leicestershire. A glorious country home surrounded by three hundred acres of land, Stanford Hall became home to the Co-operative College, which continues today as one of the preeminent places in the world to study cooperatives.

Stanford Hall now stands as a location where cooperators can become both pilgrims and practitioners. Stanford Hall in England, Var Gard in Sweden, St. Francis Xavier University in Canada, and now Kobe's Kyodo Gakuen co-op in Japan—with its exact replica of the Toad Lane store—are the crown jewels of cooperative education today.

This same commitment to education has made Migros, the innovative Swiss cooperative, that nation's largest and most famous adult education program. Through its cultural levy of 1 percent of sales, the co-op commits 45 percent to the Migros Club Schools, offering tremendous educational opportunities to thousands of Swiss cooperators. Migros had been one of the largest private businesses in Switzerland, but after reading about the commitment of the Rochdale Pioneers, the owners decided to make their business a cooperative and give it to their customers. The dreams of the Pioneers therefore led to the development of the largest retail business in Switzerland.

These noble examples embody the Pioneers' commitment to education as a tool of human freedom, and giving people the gift of education gives people a tool that serves the world's future. An investment in the type of knowledge that creates community, enhances the common good, and is meant to enrich others can only benefit both the individual and greater society. This is the purpose of the cooperative colleges, which stand as beacons of learning across the globe.

The Co-operative News

The early co-op movement was served by a number of disparate newspapers, yet needed cohesion. In 1860, Henry Pitman, brother of Isaac, the inventor of shorthand, edited *The Co-operator*, a nationally oriented paper published by the Manchester & Salford Society. *The Co-operator,* however, lost both money and the faith of the cooperators, owing to its alliance with other issues of the day. As a result, the Co-operative Congress decided to establish and support a national publication called *The Co-operative News*. First published on September 2, 1871, *The Co-operative News* is today the oldest democratically owned weekly newspaper in the world.

Despite its ultimate success, *The News* started off with difficulty. Samuel Bamford was appointed editor in 1875, at a time when the paper was heavily in debt and had a circulation of only eleven thousand. Bamford himself was a Rochdale native and a product of the Rochdale Pioneers. He had attended many of the classes given by the Pioneers and had distinguished himself in the Equitable Pioneers science and art classes. At his death, over twenty years later, the paper boasted a circulation of fifty thousand, and was a sizable and profitable enterprise. Bamford's son William became editor of *The News*; his daughter, Ann Bamford Tomlinson, was editor and founder of "Women's Outlook," a column in *The Co-operative News*.

Bamford is regarded as a key contributor to the growth and diversity of the movement because of the ideas expressed and supported in the pages of *The Co-operative News*. The weekly *Co-operative News* was the clarion call for the growing cooperative movement. Priced at a penny, it was within reach of and read by a wide cross section of the British public. During its heyday, it was one of the most influential papers in England, especially for its size.

By the end of the nineteenth century, the "learning for earning" pioneered by the co-op was provided by both local and national institutions and many other public bodies. The co-ops recognized that their contribution in this area was complete. The light lit at Rochdale in the second-floor classroom of the Pioneers now shone brightly in thousands of schoolrooms throughout Britain. Cooperatives, which had pioneered universal education programs, now looked to more specialized ways to educate their members. Assuring the future of cooperative education in an educated Britain was a much more difficult task. Co-ops could claim to have been at the forefront of overcoming inequality through education and economic action. However, by building a democratic economy with wider opportunities for working people, the co-op had lost its unique place in British society. How to reinvent itself for the twenty-first century is one of the co-op's greatest challenges. Cooperative education will be critical to strategies for rebuilding the Co-operative Movement.

Chapter 14

From Utopian Community to Garden City

Home Builder and Mortgage Banker

When the capital has accumulated sufficiently, the Society may purchase land, live upon it, cultivate it themselves, and produce any manafactures [sic] they please, and so provide for all their wants of food, clothing and houses. The society will then be called a community.
—**The Co-operator, Volume 1, May 1, 1828**
Dr. William King, Editor

The goal of the Pioneers was the creation of a cooperative community. The means to accomplish that goal were quite simple: obtain members, form a society, sell shares, open a shop, build houses, create work, and, finally, buy land and build a community for all. What stood in the Pioneers' way was the law. Until 1862, friendly societies were prevented from owning more than an acre of land, and any planner could tell you that you cannot build a Utopia on one acre.

On the other hand, the co-op's amazing growth as a grocer had stunned the nation, and co-ops were springing up in almost every town. Many of them were opening up branches and department stores, and there seemed to be no limit to the possibilities. The full-scale development of the world of retail captured the imagination of the members as they planned for greater glory. Why try anything else when the world of retail seemed such a prize?

Many of the Pioneers had been supporters of either Owenite or Chartist colonies. All of them dreamt of building a society to bring about the new world, and much of their dreams revolved around living and working in model communities.

I will not cease from mental fight
Nor let my sword sleep in my hand
Till we have built Jerusalem
In England's green and pleasant land.

Jerusalem
— William Blake

However, by the time they were in a position to do something constructive, the movement for Utopian communities was on the wane. By the 1860s the back-to-the-land yearning had passed and England's future lay with industry, not agriculture. Towns held the jobs and prosperity, as well as the squalor. What the co-op members wanted was no longer a Utopian community, but a small, neat, terraced house to call home. Town planning was now more important than idealized country living.

Engels wrote his classic description of Manchester in 1844 in *The Condition of the Working Class in England:*

(in the old town) the street, even the better ones, are narrow and winding . . . the houses dirty, old and tumble down, and the construction of the side streets utterly horrible . . . Here one is in an almost undisguised working men's quarters, for even the shops and beer houses hardly take trouble to exhibit a trifling degree of cleanliness.

It was this type of urban living that the co-op members wanted a solution to. Not in some rural Utopia, but in a nice row house.

Fortunately, the Rochdale Pioneers did not forget their roots and their commitment to community. In November of 1860, the Cooperative Land and Building Company was formed. By early 1861, the Pioneers had set up a housing and mortgage loans cooperative society and they assumed its management in 1868. In *The Co-operator* of May 15, 1867, Mr. Smithies, one of the founders, reported that the Pioneers had established a separate Building Company with a subscribed capital of four thousand pounds, and had built thirty-seven cottages. The Pioneers had the power not only to build cottages, but to buy and sell land, make bricks, supply the furniture, and do almost anything else. The Pioneers Society provided one-half of the capital, and the bulk of the Building Company's members belonged to the co-op. When the Co-operative Insurance Company (later the Co-operative Insurance Society) was formed in 1867, it set aside 50 pounds to purchase shares in the building company.

Objective 2 of the Rochdale Equitable Pioneers Society:

The building of a number of houses in which those members desiring to assist each other in improving their domestic and social condition may reside.

Just south of Rochdale's railway station off Hare Street, lie Equitable Street and Pioneer Street. These two streets were built as exact replicas of each other, each composed of two rows of the same two-story homes with small gardens in the front. In the center runs a narrow street, which clearly did not anticipate the modern car. There were approximately fifteen houses on each side of the street, making sixty houses altogether. It is quite likely that the houses were built with funds either from the Rochdale co-op or from the Co-operative Wholesale Society. Rochdale and other retail co-ops frequently sponsored this type of development to meet the needs of their members. During the past twenty years, half of Pioneer Street has been demolished to make way for a neighborhood park.

Catherine Webb, in *Industrial Co-operation*, reported that a number of the retail societies became involved in helping their members obtain housing. Nationally, by the end of the century, mortgages had been lent to finance 23,940 member houses; 8,247 houses had been built and rented to members; and 5,080 had been constructed and sold to members. The Co-operative Wholesale Society also lent money to retail societies to support home lending programs for members. Under this program, initiated in 1897, the Co-op Bank advanced to retail societies 75 percent of the cost of the property. The Bank initially set aside 250,000 pounds. The scheme proved so popular that by 1914 the Bank had provided 600,000 pounds, an amount that was over 10 percent of the total assets of the bank. In 1923 the Co-operative Insurance Society introduced its own house purchase scheme, which by 1931 covered 8,800 mortgages. In a number of cities in northern England you will find a terraced street named Co-operative, Co-operation, or Equitable. Most often, the origin of its name can be traced back to the funding and sponsorship of the local cooperative society.

In Leicester, worker cooperatives began to emerge in the late 1800s. Their presence was brought about by differences with the Co-operative Wholesale Society about employment practices, which resulted in a strike. Because they were interested in his views about cooperative workshops, the Leicester workers invited E. O. Greening, the champion of worker co-ops, to come to meet with them. Over two hundred workers agreed to join, and they asked Greening to draft a constitution. This new enterprise, known locally as "The Equity," began production in 1887, and by 1990 it employed 170 people. "The Equity" was supported by many of the consumer co-ops and became very successful.

"The Equity" next focused on a community-building project. The top floor of the factory was converted into a hall which could seat 250 people, and was to be used for social and educational purposes. There were a library, many newspapers, games, and a piano. The partners formed a number of building societies which together built sixty houses. Another worker co-op, formed in 1903, was called "The Anchor," and it was also committed to community. In the 1890s, they had purchased twenty-eight acres of land at Humberstone and built their own "garden city." The Anchor Tenant's Estate had light, airy homes, spacious gardens, and even tennis courts.

A job and partnership at The Anchor, a home on The Anchor Tenant's Estate, and shopping at the co-op shop meant that members came close to living entirely in the "cooperative commonwealth" and to following Objective 5 of the

Rochdale Equitable Pioneers Society:

> That as soon as practicable, this society shall proceed
> to arrange the powers of production, distribution,
> education and government, in other words to estab-
> lish a self-supporting home colony of united inter-
> ests, or assist other societies in establishing such
> colonies.

Another innovation was the founding of the Tenant Cooperators Limited in 1888 for the express purpose of providing dwellings for working men under a cooperative system.
At the turn of the century, this society owned a number of
estates around London. By 1909, it had built 6,600 houses. In
1907, the Lord Mayor of London opened the first cottage of
the Hampstead Tenants, a co-partnership estate. Within four
years, four hundred units of cooperative housing would be
built by Hampstead Tenants. By 1909, there were ten tenant
societies affiliated with the national organization, Co-Partnership Tenants Ltd., which raised capital and provided
technical assistance to its member organizations.

One man who had an impact on the model community
movement was the British Prime Minister, Benjamin
Disraeli, who wrote the novel *Coningsby* in 1844. Coningsby,
the protagonist of the novel, visits Manchester and looks
carefully at the industrial world he finds there:

> The next day he visits the factory of Oswald
> Millbank and describes a clear stream running
> alongside the attractive mill in this green Lancaster
> valley. About a quarter of a mile further on, appeared
> a village of not inconsiderable size, and remarkable
> from the neatness and even picturesque character of
> architecture, and the gay gardens that surrounded
> it. . . The village too could boast of another public
> building; an institute where there was a library and
> a lecture room; and a reading hall which anyone
> might frequent at certain hours, and under reason-
> able regulations.

Dean Mills, a village near Bolton, now called Barrow
Bridge, is reputed to be the inspiration for Disraeli's novel.

Industrialist Robert Gardner built a model village for the workers complete with a school and excellent housing. By 1850, the workers had started a successful co-op shop. The mills were demolished in 1913, and the remaining buildings have become a picturesque village favored by day trippers.

In his next novel, *Sybil, or The Two Nations,* published in 1845, Disraeli describes an enlightened industrialist, Mr. Trafford, who builds a model village near his mill. Disraeli's ideas influenced the first experiments in popular housing. The Bradford woolen magnate Sir Titus Salt read *Sybil* and went out and built Saltaire, a model mill community on the banks of the river Aire in west Yorkshire. Built in 1853 in the wake of the Chartist uprising, Saltaire was intended to improve conditions and avert revolt.

In *Sybil,* Disraeli describes a workmen's club similar to the Socialist Institute in Rochdale, with fifty members and subscriptions to three London papers. Disraeli spent a great deal of time in the area around Rochdale, and he was impressed by the neighborliness among the cooperators. In a later novel, *Endymion*, he captured their singular hope.

> "And I have a principle too," said the hero. "It will carry all before it, though it may not be in my time. But I am not so sure of that."
> "And what is it?" asked Endymion.
> "Co-operation."

It was in *Sybil* that Disraeli presented his description of the "two nations." He wrote:

> Two nations between whom there is no intercourse and no sympathy; who are as ignorant of each other's habits thoughts and feelings, as if they were dwellers in different zones, or inhabitants of different planets; who are formed by a different breeding, are fed by a different food, are ordered by different manners, are not governed by the same laws—the Rich and the Poor.

Mrs. Gaskell would follow a similar theme in her novel *North and South*, which describes the disparity between the people of the north and south of England.

In 1907, the president of the National Co-operative Festival, William Openshaw, said:

> Almost every variety of the necessaries of life was now Cooperatively produced but Co-operators had a long way to go before they reached the end they had in view, viz. to become a practically self-supporting and self-employing community, co-extensively with the limits of the civilized world.

Ebenezer Howard and the Garden City Movement

The concept of cooperative community continued in the creation of the Garden City Movement. Ebenezer Howard laid out this idea in his book, *Tomorrow: A Peaceful Path to Real Reform*, published in 1898. The book was reissued in 1902 under the title, *Garden Cities of Tomorrow*.

There is a very American aspect to Howard's intellectual growth. In the 1870s, he spent time in the United States, partly under doctor's orders to strengthen his lungs. He chose Nebraska with its wide open spaces to get the fresh air he needed. There, Howard was impressed by the waste of time and labor in farming due to the lack of cooperation. Later he spent time in Chicago and came under the influence of the Quakers and the humanistic philosophy of Emerson, Lowell, and Whitman.

On a second visit to the United States, in 1898, Howard was given a copy of Edward Bellamy's *Looking Backward*. Later Howard would write:

> This book graphically pictured the whole American nation organized on cooperative principles . . . The next morning as I went up to the city from Stamford Hill I realized, as never before, the splendid possibilities of a new civilization based on service to the community and not on self-interest, at present the dominant motive.

Howard would remain undeterred by *The Times'* review of *Looking Backward*. "The only difficulty is to create such a City, but that is a small matter to the Utopians."

In 1899, Howard and his supporters formed the Garden

City Association, and in 1900, a limited company, Garden City Limited, was created and authorized to sell shares. The next year, a conference to discuss the garden city concept was held near Birmingham at the model village of Bournville. Three hundred delegates attended from local councils, trade unions, and cooperative and friendly societies. Edward Cadbury, son of George Cadbury, the Quaker "king" of chocolate and cocoa, became a charter director of the Garden City Pioneer Company and a major supporter of the idea.

Another Quaker family, the Rowntrees, who had developed a housing co-op in their model village of New Earswick, sponsored a competition for the design of Letchworth. The Quaker concern for social planning moved from the employer's model village to the citizen's garden city. The Joseph Rowntree Village Trust hired the architects Raymond Unwin and Barry Parker in 1902. The two young men were greatly influenced by the ideas of John Ruskin and William Morris on visual architecture and played a major role, with Ebenezer Howard, in the creation of Letchworth and the Garden City Movement.

Letchworth, the first garden city, embodied many cooperative principles. The land is owned in common by the residents through a corporation, which they controlled democratically. The entire community was planned, and cooperation was one of its foundations. Howard proposed to the Co-operative Wholesale Society that it take over most of the retail distribution in the town. He urged firms to come to Letchworth and practice worker co-partnership, and he recommended that agricultural cooperatives and cooperative dairies run the farms. He hoped that many of the inhabitants would reside in cooperative housing.

Howard himself set a great example by living in Homesgarth, a revolutionary housing cooperative. Homesgarth was a venture of Letchworth Co-operative Houses Limited, of which Howard served for a period as chairman. To free up the work of women, the co-op was built without kitchens. All meals were held in a communal dining room. The co-op operated this way for over forty years. Today, the dining room is a quiet local pub rather than a busy intellectual cauldron. Another co-op in Letchworth was created for single women. In those days it was often difficult for single women to get mortgages, but this co-op was financed to allow women to become members.

In 1905, Garden City Tenants was established at Letchworth, created on co-partnership principles. Four hundred houses were constructed at two sites, one near the factory area and the other adjacent to the agricultural belt. Three other cooperative building societies were created in Letchworth, which together built another five hundred homes for their members.

When Letchworth opened on October 9, 1903, one thousand shareholders and guests turned out. Ebenezer Howard was fifty-three years old, and the Garden City Association numbered 2,500 members. Presiding over the formal opening ceremonies was Earl Grey, chairman of the association and an ardent, lifelong cooperator. He had been an active participant in the movement for an international cooperative body, and he was president of the first International Co-operative Alliance Congress, held in London in 1895. Grey was the first chairman of the Executive Bureau of the International Co-operative Alliance, and he was key in the development of the Canadian Co-operative Movement while Governor General of Canada. He was one of the many cooperators who played a role in the development of the Garden City Movement.

During Letchworth's early years, there was a competition for the best house built for 150 pounds or less. The cottage that won first prize was later bought by the Co-operative Permanent Building Society and used as their local office. Arthur Webb, secretary of the society, was a supporter of Howard and the Garden City Movement. Webb convinced the board to provide up to twenty thousand pounds in loans for people buying homes in the first garden city. After the first one hundred homes were financed, the society furnished other large sums. The society conducted good business while helping turn a pioneering idea into reality.

Years later Howard said that he encountered two disappointments with Letchworth. The first was that the Co-operative Wholesale Society turned down his proposal to be the main retailer, and the second was that cooperative production at Letchworth occurred on such a minimal scale. Nonetheless, Howard continued to encourage cooperatives as a major element in the development of "New Towns."

After a century of paternalistic housing schemes in Britain, there is now a movement which puts people first. The community architecture movement in Britain makes partners of housing professionals and consumers. Together they are building communities with architecture and design that meet the needs of the people who will live in them. These communities take into account the nature of people's lives and their needs for recreation, child care, employment, and shopping. The birth of the community architecture movement began with a project of three hundred households in Macclesfield, Cheshire in 1972. Once again the Northwest took the lead in the building and rebuilding of community. Britain's Community Architecture Movement maintains strong linkages to cooperatives. As Robert Owen was the patron of the Utopian communities of the nineteenth century, the Prince of Wales has become the patron of today's community architecture.

In the forward to Alan McDonald's *The Weller Way*, a book about the development of a housing cooperative begun in 1977 in a poverty district of Liverpool, the Prince of Wales wrote:

> The result was what amounted to a very attractive village nestling like an oasis in the midst of a barren urban desert. . . The value of housing Co-operatives is that they can help to provide the impetus to unleash all that potential for regeneration and ensure that people can live their lives in a more fulfilling way. . . It must surely be our aim in this country to try and create, and restore a real sense of inner city areas, based on taking account of the individual needs of residents, and by ensuring that the physical surroundings are on a suitable intimate scale to engender that community feeling. . .

Except for the passage of 150 years, the interests of the Prince of Wales differ little from those of Robert Owen when he proposed his Villages of Co-operation in 1817. Owen built his communities to allay the effects of poverty and designed them to assure sunshine, light, and room. He set aside land for vegetable gardens, buildings for schooling, canteens for good food, and halls for entertainment. Villages of Co-operation, home colonies, and housing cooperatives are all part of the quest to create community, and Rochdale's role was to create a formula for success. Today, housing cooperatives and cooperative communities lead the way in fostering community involvement and a sense of ownership and place.

As the new century began, it became clear that the old hopes of the Pioneers were being fulfilled by fresh new ideas about community and society. Building societies offices were on every High Street, and garden cities were being planned in every part of Britain. The Housing and Town Planning Act (1909) ensured quality standards of housing. Unemployment insurance was introduced in 1912, and in the same year it was followed by an early form of health insurance.

Model villages, garden cities, new towns, and planned communities all trace their origins back to the nineteenth century and Robert Owen and New Lanark. The Rochdale Pioneers, with their commitment to model community, occupied part of the continuum from Utopia to garden city. However, they ought to be viewed as having played a much more critical role in the progress towards the garden city. Prior to the Pioneers, almost all the 18th and 19th century Utopian communities were provided for by enlightened philanthropists. The Pioneers took control of the idea of community, and used their resources to build houses for their members.

The Pioneers' strength lay in their ability to create economic power from the bottom up. For the first time, working people were in control of their circumstances, and, in the case of the cooperators, sizable assets. They were also able to decide their destinies. The working poor now had a successful model which did not need to be supplemented by the rich. That ordinary people had finally found a practical model with which to build economic freedom was a breakthrough. Uniting their consumption, capital, and labor provided them with the democratic power and economic profits to carry out their dreams.

In the latter half of the nineteenth century, the Rochdale model of cooperation captivated Britain. Its economic and social success was copied in every sector of the economy. The major lesson that Ebenezer Howard learned from Rochdale was to tie citizen unity to the community. It was time to put the philanthropist out to pasture—this was the age when deference gave way to democracy. New sources of capital, in the form of building societies and cooperative organization, could provide every English man and woman with his or her castle.

Michael Cassell, author of *Inside Nationwide,* eloquently captured the impact of the Rochdale Pioneers:

> The movement was based on the vision of a Coopera-tive community, where self-help and mutual assis-tance prevailed, and on the raising of funds among—and for the use of—the working population. Demo-cratic control was the keynote and although the con-cept of Co-operation had its roots in the previous cen-tury it only began to spread rapidly after the initial success of the Rochdale experiments.

Howard was well aware of the success and the power of cooperation. In the introduction to his book, Howard states, "The town is the symbol of society—of mutual help and friendly Co-operation . . ." Were it up him, Letchworth would have been a community of extensive cooperative activity in retail, housing, and production. The reluctance of the Co-operative Wholesale Society to step forward to be the main retail partner in developing the garden city concept was a grave error. Nevertheless, Howard drew strength from the co-op model, and brought forward one of the great eras of community planning.

Lewis Mumford wrote an introductory essay for the 1965 U.S. paperback edition of Howard's book. In it Mumford wrote, "But Howard was a practical idealist like the Rochdale co-operators before him." Both the Pioneers and Howard were dedicated to dreams that worked. Charles Howarth and Ebenezer Howard were cut from the same dour cloth, and the world is a better place for it. Howarth used consumption and capital to create economic citizens, and Howard molded citi-zens and capital into creation of a democratically controlled community.

Club Row

Another form of cooperative house building was the club row. The building club was a common system in Lancashire in the late eighteenth century. A group of up to twenty people would buy land together on which to build a row of houses, which were then allocated by ballot. Club rows exist in almost every town in industrial Lancashire. Part of the original goal of the club rows was that the members would build the houses together, but it soon proved too difficult to accomplish. Even having a contractor build the homes at the same time proved complicated. In the end, the most popular method was for the club to furnish the money to the ballot winner, who then contracted directly for the building of his or her own unit.

The oldest existing club row is located at Longridge, near Preston in Lancashire. The society was established in 1793 under the guidance of the local minister. There were twenty members in the group, it cost twenty-one shillings to join, and monthly dues were ten shillings and sixpence. The society found a site suitable for twenty houses, and, with the help of the minister, raised two hundred pounds to buy the land. Each house was balloted, and the winner could either occupy the house or install a tenant. Each two-floor terraced house cost one hundred dollars to build. Within five years, all the houses had been constructed, and by 1804 the loans had been repaid and the affairs of the society terminated.

The Longridge Building Society and the club rows of Lancashire were part of the birth of both the Building Society Movement in Britain and the savings and loan associations in the United States. Early models such as Longridge were called Terminating Building Societies, because as soon as the members were housed and the leftover funds dispersed to them, the society was disbanded. Club row still stands today as a tribute to the foresight and cooperation shown by ordinary people two hundred years ago.

The societies soon gave up the roles of builder as well as banker. It became easier to gather and advance the money directly to the members who would then build their own homes. As the societies rediscovered value in playing the role of banker, they developed the concept of the permanent building society. By 1865 there were thirteen building societies in Rochdale, all committed to providing their members with the financing to build houses. These building societies became the powerhouses of finance for home-building, and they still today provide the majority of home loans in Britain.

Building Societies

The historic origins of the Building Society Movement can be traced to the creation of one in the hamlet of Deritend, in Birmingham, England, on December 3, 1781. The founding was recorded in local history, but there is no further evidence as to what happened. The era contains numerous references to building societies and club rows, and fraternal methods to furnish their members with houses.

In 1831, a group of thirty-seven men met in Frankford, Pennsylvania, to found the Oxford Provident Building Society, an idea they had gotten from the English societies. The society was necessary because banks generally would not lend money to build homes. In the American model, the person bidding the highest premium for the pooled money won the right to build the first house. In this case, the first winner's loan turned out to be a dud, but the second loan, to Comly Rich, a lamplighter, allowed him to buy a house. When Mr. Rich fell behind in his payments a few months later, another member took over the loan. In due time the loan was paid off, and thus began the Savings and Loan Movement in the United States. If you go to 4276 Orchard Street in Philadelphia, you can see the house of Comly Rich, which today is maintained as an historic monument.

The Growth of the Nationwide Building Society

In the 1880s, cooperators in Britain were well aware of the potential of the building societies. More importantly, they were deeply cognizant of the crisis in housing. Britain's towns and cities had tripled and quadrupled in population in just forty years. Demand had outstripped supply, and quality was scarce. Slums and squalor compounded the health problems of the young economy. How could hard-working cooperators find a decent place to live and the money to buy a home?

In London, a group of interested people had come together to form the Guild of Co-operators. The guild members were influenced by the success of their northern brethren, whose shops and commerce were fanning out and flourishing in every town and village in northern England. The early co-ops had branched out into wholesaling, distribution, production banking, and insurance. The guild members met on a cold January night in 1883 in a small gas-lit room on Southampton Street. Housing in Britain was a mess, and Gladstone, the Prime Minister, was consumed with problems in Ireland and elsewhere in the Empire and was unable to focus on domestic issues. If something had to be done it must be done by the people themselves. The guild members talked of encouraging thrift and making a small contribution to better living and working conditions. The challenge was immense, yet the guild members were ready. It was time to act!

The cooperators at the meeting were drawn to the ideas of Charles Cooper, who outlined to the group the concept of a building society. Cooper saw the role of the building society as financing the purchase of buildings for cooperative societies and making loans to co-op members for house construction or purchase. Six weeks later, the guild met again to review a more in-depth plan which "would aid the commercial and domestic aspirations of Co-operators." At the end of that meeting, Thomas Webb, who would become the society's first president, wrote down the guiding principles of what would become one of the world's largest and most successful building societies.

In a school exercise book that cost one penny, Webb wrote:

> The specially convened meeting decided that it was desirable to establish a Co-operative building society for the London and southern section as further aid to Co-operators and the public generally in the practice of thrift, the more comfortable housing of working people and the accumulation and profitable investment of capital.

On the evening of July 21, 1883, a small group of people gathered at the London offices of the Co-operative Wholesale

Society to witness the start of a building society to be called the Southern Co-operative Permanent Building Society which is today called Nationwide. The banking department of the Co-operative Wholesale Society agreed to be the new society's banker. One hundred years later, the society would have three million members and assets worth more than four times Britain's national income at the time of its formation.

Just weeks after the society opened for business, it made its first loan to Mr. A. O. Idle, a committed cooperator. The loan, for 120 pounds, went toward the purchase of 29 Morrison Street on the Shaftesbury Estate in Battersea. Lord Shaftesbury was the key promoter of subsidized housing estates in Britain, and he sponsored major housing reform in Parliament. The famous statue of Eros in Piccadilly Circus is actually a statue to the memory of Lord Shaftesbury's contributions to the reform movement.

The house and borrower were both looked over carefully by the board of directors. Interest was set at 5.1 percent and weekly repayments at six shillings. Mr. Idle was reportedly very pleased with the mortgage. Mr. Idle worked for the society until his death, and his three sons and one daughter followed him in his work. From this simple start emerged one of the most powerful financial institutions in Britain.

From its beginnings, Nationwide had been an innovative house lender. It went out on a limb to support the early development of Letchworth, the first garden city, and later worked with municipal councils on developing housing estates. In 1982, the society established a separate housing department to expand its role in housing development. For its entire existence, the society had been financing housing. Now it was in the business of house building, which is where the building societies had begun almost two hundred years earlier. The society was a pioneer in rebuilding the inner city and is now a leader in developing housing for people with special needs, such as the elderly and handicapped.

For most of its early years, the society maintained an institutional affinity with the British Co-operative Movement. However, a series of financial difficulties within the British retail cooperatives in the late 1960s led to the need for a clear separation. In 1970, the society changed its name to the Nationwide Building Society. What began as a humble idea among cooperators has grown into Britain's second largest building society and one of the world's unique financial institutions. At the end of 1992, Nationwide had over 6.2 million member depositors, with the most branches in the United Kingdom (730) and 35 billion pounds in assets. The handful of co-op leaders who had gathered in that cold room in London in 1883 would be proud of the progress of the idea which has housed millions.

Chapter 15

Toad Lane Yesterday and Today

Drops in separation could only fade away,
Drops in Co-operation made the ocean.
—Mahatma Gandhi

The co-op occupied the Toad Lane premises for twenty-three years. In 1867, the co-op moved up the lane into the Central Stores, a four-floor department store which the members had built to house their thriving business. The future seemed so bright that only a few looked back at the tiny store that formed the co-op's foundation. The little store became a private shop. But as the power of cooperation grew, people coming to Rochdale from all over the world would inquire about the store that had given birth to modern cooperation. When they were shown 31 Toad Lane, they saw not the "Birthplace of Co-operation," but a shoddy little shop selling canaries and bird seed. At the 1914 Co-operative Congress it was therefore resolved to raise subscriptions to buy the building. Unfortunately, World War I impeded the campaign.

By the 1920s, enough money had been raised to buy the shop, and as soon as the lease came to an end, the shopkeeper and his canaries left the building forever. The Co-operative Union and the Co-operative Wholesale Society drew up plans to restore the building to its original appearance, and the shop was officially opened as a museum in 1931. Between

1974 and 1978, the museum was closed to allow for extensive renovations and structural changes. The building is now in excellent condition, although the interior third floor was removed to provide a more open feeling to the second floor. Due to urban development and demolition, Toad Lane has gone from being the longest street in Rochdale to being the shortest. The renovated building and the Toad Lane Conservation Area was dedicated by Princess Alexandra on 13 May 1981.

The Pioneers' Museum is dedicated to displaying the history of the Co-operative Movement. Along with the building next door, the short street is a well-maintained attraction and one of the most visited sites in Rochdale's history. Visitors are strongly suggested to contact the Co-operative Union for the operating hours of the museum.

The front room of the first floor of the museum depicts the simplicity of the original store, with its meager supply of the shop's first few products: sugar, butter, flour, oatmeal, and tallow candles. Nearby are the benches where members waited to be served, the scale where their purchases were weighed, and the desk where their purchases were entered into the books of the cooperative. The rear room of the first floor depicts the history of the Rochdale Pioneers and the early leaders of the Co-operative Movement.

Originally a school and a chapel were located upstairs; the co-op took over this floor in 1849. Initially, the co-op operated a library and classroom on the first floor and a drapery and shoe repair service on the third floor. When the building was remodeled extensively in the 1970s, it was decided that the museum would be structurally safer if the third floor was removed. As a result, the second floor of the museum is a lofty and well-lit meeting and exhibition hall. Around the walls hang many historical banners and photographs. On the second floor you can also purchase a wide range of wonderful co-op souvenirs.

As the birthplace of the Pioneers, Rochdale is the Mecca of any co-op pilgrim. Percy Redfern, the great co-op historian, once stood in the store and later recounted, "So far from being dead, the Co-operative pioneers of 1844 brush past you; another deep browed, firm lipped Howarth, another slender hopeful Cooper, another Quaker-like Smithies." To open the door and enter into the tiny shop where it all began is a never-to-be-forgotten experience for any co-op activist. The original Rochdale Equitable Pioneers Society merged with the Oldham Co-operative Society in 1976 and then was absorbed into the Norwest Co-operative Society in 1982. In 1989, the Rochdale Equitable Pioneers Society was re-registered to revive the society as a supportive and promotional organization on behalf of the Pioneers Museum in Rochdale. In 1994, the society will once again be in operation.

In 1844, twenty-eight weavers gathered together to launch the modern Co-operative Movement. By 1944, the International Co-operative Alliance noted that 72 million people worldwide were members of cooperatives. When the door at 31 Toad Lane—site of the first modern cooperative—opens again on December 21, 1994, the global cooperative community will count 720 million members.

The cooperative family today is however a wider and more diverse family than the one started in 1844. The Pioneers began their co-op as a method for the little people to pool their purchasing power and effectuate savings. Today cooperatives still are the tool of the little people; however, they serve not only consumers but producers, small businesses, and nonprofits. Many of these cooperatives composed of small businesses have created big businesses such as Associated Press, F.T.D., and Best Western. With thousands of members worldwide, global cooperatives such as these provide a unique competitive edge.

Every single day, enterprising people discover the cooperative form as they look to maximize their economic needs though group effort. The taxi drivers, seamstresses, farmers and family-run corner stores in the developing world all have their co-ops to help them cut their costs and increase their opportunities. Cooperation has also become the strongest protection for independent enterprises in the developed countries to use to compete with big business. Independent grocers, hardware dealers, stationery stores, pharmacies, and florists have all built strong co-ops to build their own enterprises. Without their cooperatives, many small businesses on the High Street in England and Main Street in America would be out of business. Over 150 years later, cooperatives everywhere remain the champion of the little people in business.

The Co-operative Movement began as a working class movement in Europe intent on creating a different world. The Rochdale Pioneers made two important choices when they chose power over philanthropy and prosperity over pity. Without capital and economic independence they would be a slave to charity and beholden to a society controlled by a wealthy few. With capital they would accumulate power, and with power they could make choices and bring freedom and a democratic economy to their members.

There was philanthropy enough to ease the suffering but it would not bring independence. There was pity enough to ease the pain but it would not bring prosperity. What the Pioneers wanted was not to hope for charity but to develop a model of mutual self-help which would lift them up without others having to be brought down. They no longer wished to rely upon others to alleviate their circumstances; they intended to take matters into their own hands, and, as Holyoake said, ". . . keep them there." They saw that through cooperation they could create new wealth and develop an equitable society. They did not have to take from anyone, they just had to figure out how to keep what little they had. When millions of poor people pool their pennies they create pounds. In time, those pennies are the foundation for a rich and powerful organization. The Pioneers did just that, creating an effective model copied time and time again throughout the world. What is so unique is that the founders of each new cooperative often begin with the same enthusiasm, economic need, vision, and purpose as the Pioneers of Rochdale.

The origins of the Middle Way during the 1930s-1940s, Alternative Economics in the 1960-70s, and the Green Economy and socially responsible investing of the 1990s can all be traced to the door of Toad Lane. The Rochdale Pioneers were the first successful practitioners of a people-oriented economic model that looked beyond individual corporations to the society as a whole. Many co-ops had been tried before and most had failed. The Pioneers at Rochdale learned from earlier mistakes and history was made.

The first page of *The Best of James Herriot* begins with

Herriot's words, "The narrow street opened on to a square where we stopped. Above the window of an unpretentious grocer shop I read Darrowby Co-operative Society. We had arrived." Herriot was right, most people in the north of England identified the co-op as part of their community. For many decades the co-op stores in the north of England were models of working-class success and signified community, thrift, and self-help. These stores made a huge difference in a changing society, much as they do today in villages around the world where the local co-op *is* the community.

The Rochdale Pioneers studiously modified the cooperative model and put it into modern practice. They were ordinary people who created an extraordinary concept. Can we ever forget the cooperative legacy they left, which now affects millions? While others bombed, they built, and while others suppressed hope, they sought harmony. They knew that through cooperation they held the key to the future. Through perseverance and unity, their own meager capital, and the loyal spending of their pennies at their own store, they would gain their freedom and would never lose it. A simple idea, a committed group, and a small shop. They began a revolution that brought hope to millions and harm to none. The Pioneers gave birth to the idea of modern cooperation and the world is a better place for it!

Appendix A

Original Members of the Rochdale Equitable Pioneers Society, Limited

(This chart was revised and compiled in 1994 by Dorothy Greaves of Church View, Norden, Rochdale, from a chart originally devised by J. F. Schill Laah Copes and G. E. Crossley.)

Name	Occupation in 1844	Persuasion	Died	Aged	Buried
James Ashworth	Flannel Weaver	Chartist	April 13, 1868	76	Rochdale Cemetery
Samuel Ashworth	Flannel Weaver	Chartist	February 2, 1871	46	Rochdale Cemetery
James Bamford	Shoe Maker	Congregationalist	March 22, 1879	54	Smallbridge Church
John Bent	Tailor	Socialist	March 25, 1894	77	Rochdale Cemetery
David Brooks	Block Printer	Chartist	November 24, 1882	79	Milnrow Parish Church
John Collier	Engineer	Socialist	November 24, 1883	75	Rochdale Cemetery
William Cooper	Flannel Weaver	Socialist	October 31, 1868	46	Rochdale Cemetery
James Daly	Joiner	Socialist	December 29, 1849	37	S.S. Transit Mid Atlantic
John Garside	Cabinet Maker	Socialist	October 29, 1862	63	Rochdale Cemetery
George Healey	Silk Manufacturer	Socialist	December 27, 1899	82	Bowness, Windermere
John Hill	Carpenter	Unitarian	December 23, 1899	85	Rochdale Cemetery
John Holt	Slubber	Chartist	April 3, 1852	74	Rochdale New Burial Ground
Charles Howarth	Warper	Socialist	June 25, 1868	54	Heywood Cemetery
Benjamin Jordan	Pattern Maker	Chartist	July 16, 1904	79	Rochdale Cemetery
John Kershaw	Collier	Chartist	November 9, 1893	75	Normanton
James Maden	Flannel Weaver	Chartist	October 25, 1873	70	Bacup Cemetery
William Mallalieu	Woollen Waste Worker	Socialist	June 14, 1863	67	Ripponden
James Manock	Flannel Weaver	Chartist	March 25, 1877	79	St. Clements Church
Benjamin Rudman	Flannel Weaver	Chartist	April 19, 1876	63	Rochdale Cemetery
John Scowcroft	Hawker	Unitarian	March 11, 1870	85	Rochdale Cemetery
Joseph Smith	Woolworter	Socialist	November 16, 1888	65	Nantwich Cemetery
James Smithies	Woolsorter	Socialist	May 27, 1869	50	Rochdale Cemetery
James Standring	Flannel Weaver	Socialist	June 18, 1872	68	Rochdale Cemetery
Robert Taylor	Flannel Weaver	Socialist	July 27, 1877	77	Rochdale Cemetery
William Taylor	Power Loom Overlooker	Socialist	July 15, 1854	40	Rochdale New Burial Ground
James Tweedale	Clogger	Socialist	June 1, 1886	67	Rochdale Cemetery
Samuel Tweedale	Foreman Cotton Weaver	Socialist	October 1, 1881	73	Rochdale Cemetery
James Wilkinson	Shoe Maker	Unitarian	May 9, 1858	71	Rochdale Cemetery

APPENDIX B

Original Statutes of
the Rochdale Society of Equitable Pioneers
and
Today's International Co-operative Alliance
Co-operative Principles

The Original Statutes, Laws, and Objectives of the Rochdale Society of Equitable Pioneers, Registered October 24, 1844 in Rochdale

The objects and plans of this Society are to form arrangements for the pecuniary benefit and the improvement of the social and domestic conditions of its members, by raising a sufficient amount of capital in shares of one pound each, to bring into operation the following plans and arrangements.

The establishment of a store for the sale of provisions and clothing, etc. The building, purchasing, or erecting a number of houses, in which those members desiring to assist each other in improving their domestic and social condition may reside.

To commence the manufacture of such articles as the society may determine upon, for the employment of such members as may be without employment, or who may be badly remunerated.

That as soon as practicable, this society shall proceed to arrange the powers of production, distribution, education, and government, or in other words to establish a self-supporting home-colony of united interests, or assist other societies in establishing such colonies.

That for the promotion of sobriety a Temperance Hotel be opened in one of the society's houses, as soon as convenient.

The International Co-operative Alliance Principles
The Rochdale Principles proved to be difficult to uphold for many non-consumer cooperatives, especially worker and producer cooperatives. As a result, the International

Co-operative Alliance appointed a committee at the end of the Second World War to develop a set of principles with broader application.

The 1966 Congress of the International Co-operative Alliance, held in Bournemouth, England, approved this wording of the six Co-operative Principles:

◆ Membership of a Co-operative society should be voluntary and available without artificial or social, political, radical, or religious discrimination to all persons who can make use of its services and are willing to accept the responsibilities of membership.

◆ Co-operative societies are democratic organizations. Their affairs should be administered by persons elected or appointed in a manner agreed by the members and accountable to them. Members of primary societies should enjoy equal rights of voting (one member, one vote) and participation in decisions affecting their societies. In other than primary societies the administration should be conducted in a democratic basis in a suitable form.

◆ Share capital should only receive a strictly limited rate of interest.

◆ The economic results arising out of the operations of a society belong to the members of that society and should be distributed in such a manner as would avoid one member gaining at the expense of others. This may be done by decision of the members as follows: (a) by provision for development of the business of the corporation; (b) by provision of the common services; or (c) by the distribution among the members in proportion to their transactions with the society.

◆ All Co-operatives should make provision for the education of their members, officers, and employees and of the general public in the principles and techniques of the Co-operation, both economic and democratic.

◆ All Co-operative organizations, in order to best serve the interest of their members and their communities, should actively Co-operate in every practical way with other Co-operative at local, national and international levels.

The International Co-operative Alliance principles are once again under review. Further modifications will be introduced at the International Co-operative Alliance Congress to be held in Rochdale and Manchester in 1995. The occasion of the 100th anniversary of the founding of the International Co-operative Alliance will be used to adopt a revised set of Co-operative Principles to keep up with the rapid changes occurring in the global economy and within cooperative enterprises.

Appendix C

British Co-operative Movement
Facts and Figures for 1994

Co-operative Retail Societies

Turnover	7,290 million pounds
Trading surplus	172 million pounds
Staff	74,000
Number of societies	55
Members' benefits/dividend	28 million pounds
Number of shops	4,637 (92 superstores)
Number of members	8,188,000

The Co-operative Wholesale Society

Turnover	3.1 billion pounds
Staff	37,500
Farms	45,000 acres
Distribution centers	10
Co-op brand lines	4,500
Number of food shops	677

Co-operative Bank Group

Assets	3,398 million pounds
Staff	3,871
Branches	110
Handybanks	300
Cash-a-cheque points	2,500
Customer accounts	1.5 million pounds
Link cash machines	more than 6,000

Co-operative Insurance Society

Premium income	1,551 million pounds
Assets (held on behalf of policyholders)	11.5 billion pounds (market value)
Number of families insured	4 million
Staff	12,500
District offices	224
Surplus on life business for 1992	489 million pounds

Co-operative Travel	349 branches
Shoefayre	266 branches
Co-operative Opticians	95 practices
Co-operative Chemists	220 branches
Worker Co-operatives (UK)	1,169 (Icom Directory)

Appendix D

International Co-operative Alliance Facts and Figures for 1994

World Total 1994

725,676,982	Individuals
225	National Organizations
9	International Organizations
101	Countries

AFRICA

32	Organizations
21	Countries
19,521,735	Individuals

EUROPE

95	Organizations
35	Countries
155,705,774	Individuals

THE AMERICAS

36	Organizations
19	Countries
87,438,162	Individuals

ASIA/PACIFIC

62	Organizations
26	Countries
463,011,311	Individuals

AFRICA

Benin	56,000
Botswana	79,710
Burkina Faso	20,000
Cap Vert	20,000
Cote D'Ivoire	176,422
Egypt	4,000,000
Gambia	100,000
Ghana	1,450,000
Kenya	2,652,000
*Lesotho	788,420
Mali	4,400
Mauritius	74,821
Morocco	21,793
Niger	880,000
Nigeria	3,000,000
Senegal	2,300,000
Swaziland	11,451
Tanzania	1,351,018
Uganda	1,479,609
Zambia	907,000
*Zimbabwe	149,904

THE AMERICAS

Argentina	6,123,642
Bolivia	45,000
Brazil	3,320,000
Canada	12,000,000
Chile	581,593
Colombia	1,692,000
Costa Rica	484,347
Dominica	n/a
El Salvador	55,454
Guatemala	257,063
Honduras	137,990
Jamaica	271,719
Mexico	540,268
Panama	30,153
Paraguay	81,000
Peru	6,000
Puerto Rico	713,433
Uruguay	1,098,500
USA	60,000,000

ASIA/PACIFIC

Australia	n/a
Bangladesh	6,816,519
China	160,000,000
Fiji	9,471
India	164,000,000
Indonesia	29,000,000
Iran	4,886,909
Iraq	1,200,000
Israel	1,700,000
Japan	32,650,259
Jordan	47,435
Kazakhstan	3,700,000
Korea Rep. of	10,040,552
Kuwait	143,094
Kyrghystan	1,069,000
Malaysia	3,407,716
Mongolia	64,000
Myanmar	7,375,000
Pakistan	3,390,756
Phillipines	1,885,162
Singapore	531,363
Sri Lanka	3,400,000
Thailand	3,309,075
Turkmenistan	885,000
Uzbekistan	3,500,000
Viet Nam	20,000,000

EUROPE

Armenia	700,268
Austria	3,144,827
Azerbijan	2,000,000
Belarus	2,800,000
Belgium	2,725,967
Bulgaria	1,942,000
Cyprus	287,533
Czech Rep.	3,925,883
Denmark	1,173,774
Estonia	280,000
Finland	2,095,503
France	18,321,790
Georgia	1,700,000
Germany	6,331,000
Greece	934,863
Hungary	4,692,910
Iceland	45,968
Italy	7,134,400
Latvia	761,400
Lithuania	406,189
Moldova	1,029,400
Norway	1,218,600
Poland	15,000,000
Portugal	2,240,591
Romania	14,976,698
Russia	25,005,938
Slovak Rep.	702,516
Slovenia	20,354
Spain	2,672,205
Sweden	4,456,271
Switzerland	1,328,345
Turkey	8,204,516
UK	8,258,000
Ukraine	11,000,000
Ex-Yugoslavia	n/a

Indirect members

Bibliography

A *Pioneer Looks at 1944*, Co-operative Wholesale Society, Manchester, 1946.

Ackroyd, Peter, *Introduction to Dickens*, New York: Ballantine Books, 1991.

Acland, Arthur H. Dyke, *The Education of Citizens*, Manchester: Central Co-operative Board, c. 1920.

Alderson. Caroline, *The South Pennines*, Standing Conference of the Pennine Authorities, c. 1990.

Allen, Agnes, *The Co-operative Story*, Manchester: Cooperative Union, 1953.

Allen, George and Unwin, *One Man's Vision*, York: Ebor Press, 1954.

Backstrom, Philip N., *Christian Socialism and Co-operation in Victorian England*, London: Croom Helm, 1974.

Bagley, J. J., *Lancashire Diarists: Three Centuries of Lancashire Lives,* Chichester, 1975.

Bailey, Jack, *The British Co-operative Movement*, London: Hutchinson and Co., 1955.

Benevolo, Lenardo, *The Origins of Modern Town Planning,* Cambridge, Massachusetts: M.I.T Press, 1967.

Bonner, Arnold, *British Co-operation*, Manchester: Co-operative Union, 1970.

Böök, Sven Åke, *Cooperative Values in a Changing World*, Geneva: International Cooperative Alliance, 1992.

Brontë, Charlotte, *Shirley*. London: Penguin Books, 1974.

Brown, W. Henry, *Brighton's Cooperative Advance: A Story of Sussex Pioneering*, Manchester: Co-operative Union, 1939.

Brown, W. Henry, *The Rochdale Pioneers*, Manchester: Co-operative Union, 1944.

Button, John, *The Green Guide to England*, London: Green Print, 1989.

Cassell, Michael, *Inside Nationwide: One Hundred Years of Co-operation*, London: Nationwide Building Society, 1984.

Clarke, Allen, *The Effects of the Factory System*, London: Grant Richards, 1899.

Co-operative Life, London: Cooperative Printing Co., 1889.

Co-operative Union, *The Rochdale Equitable Pioneers' Society*, Manchester: 1967.

Cole, G.D.H., *A Century of Co-operation*, Manchester: Co-operative Wholesale Society, c. 1945.

Cole, John, *Conflict & Co-operation: Rochdale and the Pioneering Spirit*, Littleborough: George Kelsall Publishing, 1994.

Cole, John, *Down Poorhouse Lane: The Diary of a Rochdale Workhouse*, Littleborough: George Kelsall Publishing, 1984.

Cole, Margaret, *Beatrice Webb*, New York: Harcourt, Brace and Company, 1946.

Cooper, William, *History of the Rochdale District,* London: Holyoake & Co., no date.

Davies, Margaret Llewelyn, ed., *Maternity: Letters from Working Women*, London: Anchor Press, 1978.

Davies, Margaret Llewelyn, ed., *Life As We Have Known It*, London: Hogarth Press, 1931.

Davies, T. C., *A Brief History of the Co-operative Wholesale Society Bank*, Manchester: Co-operative Wholesale Bank, 1930.

Deans, James, *Co-operative Memories*, Manchester: National Co-operative Publishing Society, 1922.

Disraeli, Benjamin, *Coningsby*, London: Penguin Classics, 1989 (1844).

Disraeli, Benjamin, *Sybil*, London: Penguin Classics, 1985 (1845).

Disraeli, Benjamin, *Endymion*, London: Longmans, Green, and Co., 1880.

Donnachie, Ian and Hewitt, George, *Historic New Lanark,* Edinburgh: Edinburgh University Press, 1993.

Elliot, Sydney R., *Co-operative Store-Keeping*, Edinburgh: Riverside Press, 1925.

Elliott, Sydney R., *The English Cooperatives*, New Haven: Yale University Press, 1937.

Engels, Friedrich, *The Condition of the Working Class in England*, London: Penquin Books. 1987 (1845).

Flanagan, Desmond, *A Centenary Story of the Co-operative Union of Great Britain and Ireland*, Manchester: Co-operative Union, 1969.

Freethy, Ron and Marlene, *Inland Lancashire*, Edinburgh: John Donald Publishers, 1991.

Gaffin, Jean and Thomas, David, *Caring and Sharing*, Manchester:

Garnett, R. G., *A Century of Co-operative Insurance*, London: George Allen & Unwin, 1968.

Garnett, R. G., *Co-operation and the Owenite Socialist Communities in Britain 1825-45*, Manchester: Manchester University Press, 1972.

Garratt, Morris, *Samuel Bamford: Portrait of a Radical,* Lancashire: George Kelsall, 1992.

Gaskell, Elizabeth, *Mary Barton*, London: Aldine Press J.M. Dent & Son, 1971 (1848).

Gaskell, Elizabeth, *North and South*, London: J. M. Dent, 1993 (1855).

Greenwood, Abraham, *The Education Department of the Rochdale Equitable Pioneers' Society: Its Origin and Development*, Manchester: Co-operative Printing Society, 1877.

Haddington, Peter, *Around Manchester Guide*, Cheshire: Willow Publishing, 1990.

Hadfield, Alice Mary, *The Chartist Land Company*, Devon: Latimer Trend & Co., 1970.

Hall, F. and Watkins, W. P., *Co-operation*, Manchester: Co-operative Union, 1937.

Hall, Fred, *Sunnyside*, Manchester: Co-operative Printing Society, 1935.

Harrison, Molly, *People and Shopping*, Toronto: General Publishing Co., 1975.

Hayes, Cliff, *Stories and Tales of Old Lancashire*, Manchester: Printwise Publications, 1991.

Herriot, James, *The Best of James Herriot*, New York: Reader's Digest Association, 1982.

Hill, Patricia M., McGrath, Mary Jean, and Reyes, Elena, *Cooperative Bibliography*, Madison, Wisconsin: University of Wisconsin Extension, 1981.

Chushichi, Tsuzuki, ed., *Robert Owen and the World of Co-operation*, Tokyo: University of Tokyo Press, 1992.

Holyoake, George J., *Thirty-Three Years of Co-operation in Rochdale*, London: Truber & Co., 1882.

Holyoake, George J., *Manual of Co-operation*, New York: John B. Alden Publisher, 1885.

Holyoake, George J., *The History of Co-operation*, London: T. Fisher Unwin, 1906.

Howard, Ebenezer, *Garden Cities of Tomorrow*, Cambridge, Massachusetts: M.I.T. Press, 1965, (1902, 1898).

Howard, Ebenezer, *Lifeline 18*, Bucks: Shire Publishing, 1973.

International Co-operative Alliance, *Review of International Co-operation,* vol. 86, no. 2, 1993.

International Co-operative Alliance, *Review of International Co-operation,* vol. 86, no. 3, Annual Report 1993.

Johns, Alessa, "Engendering Utopias: Examples from Mid-Eighteenth-Century England" in *Transformations of Utopia*, Paul Alkon, Roger Gaillard, and George Slusser, eds., New York: AMS Press, in press.

Kagawa, Toyohiko, *Brotherhood Economics,* London: Harper & Brothers, 1936.

Kingsley, Charles. *Alton Locke: Tailor and Poet*. London: Collins' Clear-Type Press, 1851.

Kingsley, Mrs. Charles, *Charles Kingsley: His Letters and Memories of His Life,* New York: Charles Scribner's Sons, 1890.

Knevitt, Charles and Wates, Nick, *Community Architecture*, London: Penguin Press, 1987.

Knevitt, Charles, *Space on Earth*, London: Thames Methuen, 1985.

Lambert, Paul, *Studies in the Social Philosophy of Co-operation*, Manchester: Co-operative Union, 1963.

Lancaster, Bill, *Radicalism, Co-operation and Socialism*, Leicestershire: Leicester University Press, 1987.

Lawron, David, *Village Co-operation*, Manchester: Wholesale Society's Printing Works, 1906.

Longmate, Norman, *The Hungry Mills*, London: Temple Smith, 1978.

MacFayden, Dugald, *Sir Ebenezer Howard and the Town Planning Movement*, Manchester: Manchester University Press, 1970.

Madams, Julia P., *The Story Re-Told*, Manchester: Co-operative Union, 1928.

Marshall, Allan, *In the Beginning and Later*, Rochdale: Towers of Rochdale, c. 1992.

McCabe, Joseph, *George Jacob Holyoake*, London: Watt's & Co., 1922.

McDonald, Alan, *The Weller Way*, London: Weller Streets Publishing Company, 1986.

Mercer, T. W., *Co-operation is Prophet*, Manchester: Co-operative Union, 1947.

Morris, Max, ed., *From Cobbett to the Chartists 1815-1848*, London: Lawrence & Wishart, 1951.

Nettlefold, J. S., *Practical Housing*, Letchworth: Garden City Press, 1893.

Nicholson, Isa, *Our Story*, Manchester: Co-operative Union, 1908.

Parker, Florence E., *The First 125 Years*, Chicago: Cooperative League of the USA, 1936.

Paul, Leslie A., *Story Without End*, Manchester: Co-operative Union, 1937.

Pollard, Sidney and Salt, John, *Robert Owen, Prophet of the Poor*, Lewisburg, Pennsylvania: Bucknell University Press, 1971.

Potter, Beatrice, *The Co-operative Movement in Great Britain*, London: Swan Sonnenschein & Co., 1893.

Priestley, John H., *The History of Ripponden Co-operative Society Limited*, Halifax, England: F. King & Sons, 1932.

Purdom, C. B., *The Garden City*, Letchworth: Temple Press Printers, 1913.

Redfern, Percy, *Co-operation for All*, Manchester: Co-operative Union, 1914.

Redfern, Percy, *The Consumers Place in Society*, Manchester: Co-operative Union, 1920.

Redfern, Percy, *The Story of the C.W.S.*, Manchester: Co-operative Wholesale Society Limited, 1944.

Redfern, Percy, *John T.W. Mitchell: Pioneer of Consumers' Co-operation*, Manchester: Co-operative Union, 1924.

Robertson, William, *Rochdale: The Birthplace of Modern Co-operation*, Manchester: Co-operative Printing Society Limited, 1892.

Roper, Robert Stephenson, *The Co-op Chapel of Rochdale*, England: Quickfit Products, 1993.

Scott, Alexander, *A Little Story About a Big Idea*, Glasgow: Civic Press, 1835.

Scott, R.D.H., *The Biggest Room in the World: A Short History of the Manchester Royal Exchange*, London: Royal Exchange Theatre Trust, 1976.

Scott, Sarah, *Millenium Hall*, New York: Viking Penguin Inc., 1986. (First published in Great Britain by J. Newberry, 1762.)

Stoddast, A. and Clayton W., *Foundations*, Manchester: Co-operative Union, 1916.

The Hungry Forties: A Collection of Letters, New York: Scribner, Armstrong, and Company, 1877.

Turner, William, *Riot! The Story of East Lancashire Loom Breakers in 1826*, Lancashire: Lancashire County Books, 1992.

Twigg, H. J., *An Outline History of Co-operative Education*, Manchester: Co-operative Union, 1924.

Unwin, Raymond, *Co-Partnership in Housing*, London: Co-partnership Publishers Limited, 1909.

Vicinus, Martha, *Edwin Waugh*, Lancashire: George Kelsall, 1984.

Walton, John K., *Wonderlands by the Waves*, Lancashire: Lancashire County Books, 1992.

Watkins, William P., *Co-operative Principles: Today and Tomorrow*, Manchester: Co-operative Union, 1986.

Watkins, William Pascoe, *The International Co-operative Alliance 1895-1970*, London: Church Gate Press, 1970.

Waugh, Edwin, *Lancashire Sketches*, Manchester: John Heywood Printing, 1881.

Webb, Catherine, *The Woman with the Basket*, Manchester: Co-operative Wholesale Society's Printing Works, 1927.

Welty, Joel David, *Rochdale Ethics: Foundation of Cooperative Culture*, Ann Arbor, Michigan: North American Students of Cooperation, 1985.

Windsor, Davis Burns, *The Quaker Enterprise*, London: Frederick Muller Limited, 1980.

David J. Thompson was born in Blackpool, England, in 1942 and emigrated to the United States in 1962. In the late 1960s, he became involved in the civil rights and anti-war movements. Looking back on the crowd of over a quarter of a million people gathered for the 1970 San Francisco Peace March, he came to the conclusion that if people were active in co-ops, a better society could be built. Since then he has committed himself to building a cooperative economy.

For the past twenty years, David has been active in the cooperative sector in the United States. He co-chaired California's efforts to win passage of the legislation that established the National Cooperative Bank in 1978 and the Center for Cooperatives at the University of California in 1987. David was Director of the Western Region of the National Cooperative Bank and later the Director of International Relations for the National Cooperative Business Association. He is now principal of Thompson Consulting. David has written over 100 articles about cooperatives, and his work has been published in six books and four languages. He serves on the board of REI, America's largest consumer cooperative (1.3 million members) and the Davis Food Co-op. He is president of the Twin Pines Cooperative Foundation.

David has collected the world's largest private library on cooperatives. Much of his collection has been gathered from sources in Britain, and it is from much of this original literature that he studied and culled the material to write this book.

David's family on both sides is descended from generations of Lancashire folk. In 1844, his great-great-great grandfather was a hand loom weaver working in the Lancashire village of Hoghton, eighteen miles from Rochdale. By the 1860s, both maternal and paternal families were members of cooperatives. Both sides of his family have been of public service to Lancashire. His grandfather, John Clayton, served on the Oldham Town Council; his uncle, Peter Thompson, served as chairman of the Oswaldtwistle and Church Urban District Council; and a cousin, Pat White, works for the Rochdale Metropolitan Borough Council. Carrying her own family tradition, his wife, Ann Evans, was Mayor of Davis, California, a "City of Cooperatives" and the first manager of the State of California's Cooperative Development Program.

From David's first day in the world, the co-op milkman delivered to the family's door. The dividend earned at the co-op helped buy the house, his first suit, and the annual Christmas presents and dinner. David and every member of his family have all worked for the "co-op."

His strength of purpose is derived from the contribution his family made to the building of Lancashire. He was taught to honor those who make history and to respect the unselfish pioneers who left behind a better world. The best part of this world was created by people like the Pioneers who nurtured it for future generations. He is glad that his daughter Hatley Rose can live in a world of cooperatives and cooperation.